What It Takes
to Be a Doctor

For Sankalp, Shreya and Sneha,
with love

Pseudonyms have been used in this book and other details altered where necessary to protect the identity and privacy of people mentioned.

WHAT IT TAKES TO BE A DOCTOR: AN INSIDER'S GUIDE
First published in Australia in 2018 by
Simon & Schuster (Australia) Pty Limited
Level 4, 32 York Street, Sydney, NSW 2000

10 9 8

New York Amsterdam/Antwerp London Toronto Sydney New Delhi
Visit our website at www.simonandschuster.com.au

A catalogue record for this
book is available from the
National Library of Australia

Cover design: Jacalin King
Cover image: Shutterstock
Typeset by Midland Typesetters, Australia
Printed and bound in Australia by Griffin Press

ISBN: 9781925791730

The paper this book is printed on is certified against the Forest Stewardship Council® Standards. Griffin Press holds chain of custody certification SCS–COC-001185. FSC® promotes environmentally responsible, socially beneficial and economically viable management of the world's forests.

Contents

Contents

Foreword

Professor Michelle Leech

What It Takes to Be a Doctor is a book that needed to be written. There may be people who are born to be doctors, although I suspect that almost all humans have an infinite capacity to become almost all things. Others grow into the medical role and become the most natural care givers in the world. Problem-solving scientists with big hearts.

The number of doctors in Australia is now well above the OECD average and we suffer more from maldistribution and perverse 'super-specialisation' than shortage. Although thousands of capable students dream of becoming doctors, the places in medical schools must be limited or capped to avoid this oversupply.

Medical schools in Australia, down to the last, are unified in their recognition of the importance of empathy and compassion in those they select and train to be doctors. For all courses, and medicine is no exception, universities work hard to calibrate and recalibrate the balance between meritocracy and equity of access, with the full understanding that eligibility on academic 'merit' is even now still socially determined.

The demand for a place in medical school in Australia is unprecedented and rising steeply each year. Medical student places are capped for important reasons. When a medical student graduates they are not immediately ready to practise independently but must undertake a period of training. The current oversupply of medical graduates is creating a problem wherein training opportunities, especially in rural Australia, are not keeping pace with graduate numbers.

Each year medical school deans lament with the thousands of talented, highly intelligent and no doubt empathic young high school students or graduates who have missed out on a place in medicine. For those who are successful in this crucible, the collision between high academic achievement and a working life that is predominantly about unglamorous service can be discordant.

Dr Ranjana Srivastava is an oncologist, Fulbright Scholar, award-winning writer and presenter and has now turned her sensitive and incisive lens to this important issue and provided a platform for medicine aspirants to explore their motivation and to courageously face external and parental expectation.

Many cautionary tales unfold but so too the joys, virtues and unending rewards that come from embracing this service. She celebrates the enormous breadth and opportunity within medical practice at the same time as exploring the practical constraints of training and parenting. She is unflinching in her discussion of the pervasive mental health issues that arise in doctors, medical students (and I would argue) all healthcare professionals, emergency workers and anyone working in any field at the coal-face of humanity.

This book creates an important opportunity for discussion and self-examination, a moment to pause and consider the next steps with more information in hand. It is an excellent basis for discourse between students and parents or students and career counsellors. This is a book as much for parents as it is for aspiring medical students.

There may be many parents who, in spite of the prestige, lament in hindsight that their children may have had an easier life. Equally there will be parents who feel certain that their children will thrive in the medical profession. In the final analysis, humans are highly adaptable and can survive any vocational error. In my roles as physician, scientist, teacher, mother, and head of a medical course, I have mostly seen the joys of a career well chosen, but equally I have seen many suffer.

However, choosing wisely and from one's true heart space, if one can find it, will lead to a person who thrives within that vocation. Thriving young doctors are so much more capable of caring for self, others and our communities. This is what each person, each patient and each community deserves.

For every place available in medical school, there are on average between 10 to 15 eligible applicants. A defensible process must somehow select one person from this eligible 15. It was recognised long ago that problem solving, accountability, integrity, service orientation, kindness and empathy were as valuable as intellectual capability. Which of these can be measured? It has been written that there is beggary (something lacking) in that which can be reckoned or measured – nowhere more true than in this instance.

Having taught and worked with over 25 graduating cohorts of medical students and met and spoken with many hundreds of students who have missed out on a place in medicine over the decades, I would say that the world is full of capable, intelligent and compassionate young people from all cultures and backgrounds. There are yet thousands more people who are capable of doing medicine than can be selected. I am a physician–scientist who has measured many molecules over the years. I like to think that I can feel empathy in another human being – especially over time or when interacting with them in a range of circumstances. I think I know it when I see it. I still don't know how to measure it.

This book offers practical help for those who aspire to study medicine and for those who do not have the words or courage to explain that they do not. Dr Srivastava examines the changing face of medicine, the daily reality of practice and service, the high human cost and at the same time embraces the energising challenges of medicine. Written from the perspective of someone who has found their true north in the profession, she shares stories of those for whom the practice of medicine has been less than rewarding. The intercalation of anecdote, fact and wise insight is, as always with Dr Srivastava's writing, beautifully calibrated.

Professor Michelle Leech is Deputy Dean at the Monash Faculty of Medicine, Nursing and Health Science. She is a physician–scientist and head of the medical course at Monash University. She has taught medical students for three decades. She is a rheumatologist at Monash Health.

Introduction

'Let food be thy medicine and
medicine be thy food.'
Hippocrates

So, you want to be a doctor! Congratulations for picking up this book to find out more. I have been a doctor for twenty years and in that time I have had the pleasure of talking to many high school students and parents about life as a doctor. I must say that the questions from students have become increasingly sophisticated and I am left marvelling at the thoughtfulness, poise and curiosity of people so young. Along the way, I have also worked closely with school counsellors, hospital welfare officers and, of course, doctors of all ages. Their observations have provided rich insights into medicine with all its ups and downs. This book is my attempt to answer the most common questions people have about a career in medicine with the honesty, clarity and engagement they merit. Although I am unquestionably biased towards a career in medicine, there should always be room to discuss the challenges and concerns and hope for better.

My eyes light up when I hear that someone wants to be a doctor. For me, there is meaning, privilege and joy in a job that I would wish upon everyone. Because I didn't pursue my other (misguided) choice of engineering, there is one less civil engineer in the world, which also has better bridges and roads that lead somewhere! For me, medicine has been the right choice but, as I have come to realise, this hasn't been the case for many others. Even if you think you want to be a doctor, there are reasons it may not be right for you. Having not succeeded at getting into medicine at your first attempt, you may be wondering whether it is still the right career decision. Or you wouldn't even be considering it were it not for the desire of your parents to have a doctor in the family.

Students come to me with all sorts of questions. Some are practical, others are curious, and some philosophical. They are all meaningful. I am impressed by the depth of the questions and how hard young people are thinking about their future. I can't say I was as thoughtful or deliberate but then the stakes seem different too. The pressure to excel at exams, achieve ever-greater heights and accumulate wealth is palpable. Students are measured by their scores. There is far more parental involvement and guidance than ever before, not all of it healthy. Social media sites like Facebook and Instagram multiply the pressure by suggesting what young people should think, do and aspire to.

On the other hand, a school leaver today has many more choices than my peers had. The first time I met someone who came near the top of her high school and chose not to pursue medicine (she studied environmental science) was a shock, but now the phenomenon is a little more common. More medical courses are becoming postgraduate degrees, which means that students must complete an undergraduate degree before applying to study medicine. This has two purported benefits – it allows students to experience a broad education before deciding, and it allows for four extra years of maturity, which turn out to be critical when dealing with matters of life and death.

However, even though university students have a wide amount of choice during an undergraduate degree, the majority opt for a pre-med course to enhance their chances of getting into medicine. Some undergraduate health sciences courses offer guaranteed entry into postgraduate medicine by maintaining a robust grade point average. Many students feel that, if they truly pursued an interest in history, philosophy, or music, they would miss out on precious years of preparing for medical school.

Thus, while most high school students need not think about preparing for medical school until their undergraduate degree is complete, the reality is that they decide well beforehand and choose their high school subjects accordingly. Educators say that the pressure to decide seems to be coming earlier and earlier, a combination of personal expectations fuelled by anxious parents and a competitive society.

If you are a student in high school pondering your career decisions, or indeed a parent of such a child, I hope this book will provide you an insider's honest perspective of medicine. From the outside, being a doctor seems like a glamorous career, but needless to say it's not all so. I hope to take you inside the highs and lows of medicine, the practicalities and the things that I never thought about but wish I had.

Courses like law, science or arts can be an entry point into other careers. For example, as many as half the students who study law don't end up as practising lawyers. Many law graduates will enter politics, business, or academia. Other graduates can't find available jobs.

A degree in science or arts offers diverse opportunities in all kinds of industry. I know a music graduate who plays in a popular jazz band and one who coordinates music therapy at a meditation retreat. A science student I know became a science editor at a prominent newspaper, while her roommate is the chief scientist of a laboratory. A journalist started off studying economics but found herself drawn to editing the college journal. You can probably think of people in your own family who ended up in work they didn't study for.

In contrast, medicine is narrow. By studying medicine, you are committing to becoming a doctor. Some medical graduates enter research, administration, or work for the government or pharmaceutical industry, but by and large most medical graduates become practising doctors. Medical educators stress this to avoid the risk of mismatched expectations.

Making a decision to enter a profession should not be taken lightly, but in life you will make many important decisions and not get them right the first time. Studying medicine is such an all-consuming journey that it's worthwhile having some bearings. What I hope to give you through my lived experience of being a doctor is the tools to help you decide whether this journey is for you.

1

A little bit about me

> 'As to diseases, make a habit of two things –
> to help, or at least to do no harm.'
>
> Hippocrates

If I were reading a book about whether becoming a doctor is right for me, I'd ask to know more about who was writing it. So let me tell you a little about myself. I was born in Australia to Indian parents and grew up in India, the United Kingdom and the United States in a family that prized academic achievement. However, there were no doctors in our family and I was hardly exposed to them. The little I did see of doctors as a child didn't leave me with any strong impression that I wanted to follow in their footsteps. While my family believed in the advantages of higher education, becoming a doctor, or pursuing any specific career for that matter, was not something my family openly discussed. It was simply expected that my brother and I would go to university and figure out what to do. I now meet children who are determined to become doctors; I was so neutral towards the concept for practically all of high school that I am somewhat surprised I got there.

When I graduated from a public high school in the United States in the early 1990s, there were fewer visible career choices. I arrived in Australia shortly afterwards and quickly saw that if you had done very well in high school, it was expected that

5

you would study medicine or law. In fact, people assumed that this is what you would *want* to do. Other popular courses were science, arts, engineering, teaching and nursing; and then there was vocational training for students looking to enter a trade. Like today, each course had a different mark and different entry criteria. I was very keen to study medicine, but unfortunately didn't have the grades to safely get in. I was rejected in the first round of offers, then in the second round of offers and, just as I had given up, was offered an interview at one university. It was the middle of a very hot summer and I was still settling into my uncle's home in Australia. Thinking about attending university in the United States, I had done some interviews but they were informal ones, a 'getting to know you' type, where an alumnus had met me for a chat about campus life.

So, when I was invited to interview at an Australian medical school, I didn't realise the significance of the occasion. I had made a new friend who dropped me off to my interview. I arrived wearing a T-shirt and shorts and my heart sank when I saw the rows of formally dressed students in skirts and wearing ties lined up in the waiting room.

I thought I had lost my chance right there and kicked myself for not having been more prepared. But back in those days, there was no internet (gasp!), no mobile phone (gasp again!) and the letter sent by post had been short on explanation. There I was, neither dressed nor rehearsed for the interview that seemed like the make-or-break event of my life.

I am cautious by nature, but now I felt there was nothing to lose. When my turn came, I was greeted by three interviewers. They asked me numerous questions to get a sense of who I was and what I cared about. It wasn't like classroom questioning about subject matter and, perhaps because I had already decided that I wasn't going to get into medicine, I settled into a comfortable conversation. I rued that the chance to impress my interviewers had passed, but there was nothing I could do about that. And while I wouldn't recommend this as a trick, this realisation turned out to be very freeing for me. I felt that I could answer their questions with honesty and without second-guessing what they were thinking about me. (I already knew!) I made plenty of eye contact, engaged, and gave them a sense of the person behind the not-so-stellar marks.

Soon, my twenty minutes ended and I was out. The deadline came and went. I never heard back. I was bitterly disappointed. Being on the grounds of the medical faculty had really lit my desire to study medicine.

So, as I said, if you did well at high school back then, you chose one of the professional courses. My second choice was engineering. Let me confess, I had no interest in being an engineer. I had never thought about it as a career, never spent a day talking to an engineer, and didn't really have the kind of grasp of the sciences I'd need to do well at engineering. My parents didn't tell me to do it either and my high school counsellor had never mentioned it. Everything that engineering required made it a bad fit for me, but I didn't stop to think about this beyond telling myself that if I didn't get into medicine, I'd somehow make myself like engineering because it was a prestigious course. Misguided, I know. Do students still make this mistake? Yes. I was admitted to engineering and beyond fleeting relief felt nothing.

Finally, the day dawned when I had to enrol in engineering. I felt unexcited, even apprehensive about what I had committed to, but followed the instructions automatically.

I called the then central admissions office to ask about where to appear for enrolment. I will never forget the ensuing conversation with the kindly lady who answered the phone.

'What course are you enrolling in today, dear?'

'Engineering.'

There was silence, followed by, 'You mean medicine.'

'No, I didn't get into medicine.'

'But that's what I have in front of me.'

Regret welled up inside me and I mustered the courage to say to the stranger on the phone, 'Please don't play games with me. I applied to medicine but I didn't make it.'

'But you did, dear.'

My stunned silence must have simultaneously confused her and melted her heart, because on a madly busy day, she offered, 'Wait for a moment. I will get someone to double-check.'

Her colleague came on the line and was much more straightforward.

'I can confirm you have been offered a place to study medicine.'

'I told you so!' the friendly lady chirped. 'Now go out there and celebrate!'

In complete bewilderment, I called the faculty of medicine. On the day of enrolment, everyone was frantic. The lady who took my call said it was odd that I had not received a letter of confirmation and that she wasn't in a position to help me yet. I didn't want to miss out on enrolling in engineering but was made to wait at home (there were no mobile phones then, remember!) for the next four hours before someone confirmed the happy news that indeed I had been given a place in medicine – as I was to discover years later, the very last place.

Due to an administrative delay, my letter of acceptance arrived in the mail days later. That yellowing piece of paper is one of my favourite possessions.

Later that day as I enrolled in medicine, I joined the queue of aspiring doctors. Here, I met countless students who were all obviously brighter and better than me because no one had endured the nail-biting wait that I had. I couldn't have known it at the time, but over the next few years some of them would drop out, switch courses, become disillusioned, commit suicide, become depressed, and discover that the reality of medicine was different from what they had dreamed.

In that queue, I also met many people who would go on to a fulfilling career in medicine, would love and cherish their job, and celebrate the day they got into medicine. I made friends who have stayed friends. We have watched each other marry, have children and followed the ups and downs in the lives of our families. When things are tough at work, no one quite understands the nuances like another doctor. A loyal circle of fellow doctors feels like a home within a home.

I am now a cancer specialist, also known as an oncologist. I chose to do oncology because I think it provides the right blend of the art and science of medicine, something that was important to me. I have specialised further as a geriatric oncologist, which means I mostly look after very elderly patients, in their eighties and nineties, with cancer and accompany them on the journey from their diagnosis to the time they get better, or, sadly, till they die. Looking after patients for many years is a great way to learn things about other people, yourself and medicine.

First, I am privy to an intimate view of the experiences my patients and their loved ones endure as they tackle a serious illness. These experiences are good, bad, uplifting and frightening and I have had to learn to cope with them all.

Second, since my job involves working closely with many doctors in the hospital and in the community, I have developed a good sense of what different doctors do. It's clear that just as patients face illness differently, doctors practise medicine differently. It is said that the good doctor treats the disease but the wise doctor treats the person with the disease.

One of the commonest questions I am asked about my job is whether it's sad. Well, it's certainly a job that makes me stop to think and reflect and sometimes it's sad too, but mostly I feel very privileged. My patients are very sick and in need of a lot of care, compassion and empathy. My job involves not only prescribing the right medicines for them, but also caring for them as people. It means knowing when they last had a fever, but also that every time they come into hospital, they are really worried about who will feed their dog or water their roses.

For every patient, I hold multiple concerns because I have learnt that illness doesn't happen just to one person, it has an impact on family and friends. Keeping this in mind, I have tried to play a broader role in society through volunteering on missions abroad, contributing to government committees and educating and empowering communities, through my writing and public speaking, to look after their own health.

The capacity to make a difference to people's lives in so many ways is what I most enjoy about being a doctor. Twenty-five years after the fateful day I was offered a place in medicine, I still thank my stars. For me, becoming a doctor was the right decision. And I hope that reading this book will help you decide if it is right for you.

2

Why do you want to be a doctor?

'Wherever the art of medicine is loved,
there is also a love of humanity.'

Hippocrates

I have lost count of how many times I have asked this question, a standard inclusion on interview panels from the time students apply to medical school to the points where they progress through medicine's higher ranks (when the question is modified but the intent is the same). You might think that anyone who aspires to study medicine has thought about this question deeply, but in fact many students haven't. By far the commonest answer is, 'Because I want to help people.' This is of course an important intention but it can be realised in hundreds of ways that don't involve being a doctor, which I will return to.

Other students who have performed well in school say that either they or their parents think they should give medicine a try, usually because of the prestige associated with being a doctor. Parents who may not have finished university themselves, left promising careers in their home country, or harboured a dream to become a doctor, may subtly or pointedly put pressure on their child to study medicine. On the other hand, you may be the child of professional parents, including doctors, who want you to follow in their footsteps.

School and university teachers may remark on your 'potential', which makes you feel like you must live up to that potential.

Studying medicine seems one sure-fire way of doing this and making a lot of people happy in one hit! But the best doctors are those who search their own hearts for a response. They listen to counsel but don't follow every word, instead setting themselves the task of thinking long and hard about where their true interest lies. They pay attention to their subjects in school and ask themselves what they like.

Does human biology grab your attention and you can spend hours immersed in it, or is it something you slog at because you 'should'? Do you enjoy talking to people and listening to their concerns or would you rather spend time quietly solving a mathematical problem or tinkering with a machine? You might be smart and articulate and find the cut and thrust of the school debating team or politics club the most interesting thing about school. Or you do well at science but your passion lies in conjuring architectural wonders. Your parents might run a business and you feel you have a knack for business, or you might have a parent who is a doctor and know that, much as you respect her for it, it's not your cup of tea. Her young daughter made this clear to my doctor friend when she said, 'I want to get the marks you did but not to study medicine.'

Seeking out work experience is a good way to learn about the day to day work of a doctor. It is the quickest way of dispensing with the myth that all medicine is glamorous! The stuff on television shows may look alluring, but much of real-life medicine is the opposite. Medicine involves long hours, difficult encounters and wicked dilemmas. It involves working with numerous people, coordinating many tasks, and taking responsibility for a range of decisions.

It requires a lot of mental and emotional energy and it's practically impossible to leave your work at work. Dealing with human lives means that human emotions follow you home and I don't know that any doctor can completely compartmentalise things between work and home. But then again, this is what makes medicine a joy and a privilege – the ability to accompany patients during difficult times, the power to keep them well, the knowledge to make them better. However, it's important to acknowledge that these things are not within the sole domain of doctors.

Some of the people who I think make the greatest difference to patients are nurses and allied health providers like physiotherapists, occupational therapists, speech pathologists and social workers. Pharmacists are routinely ranked among the most trusted members of society. Psychologists are playing an increasingly important role helping people cope with life's challenges. I work closely with all these people and I can tell you that, without them, patients would struggle even under the care of the best doctor.

Each one of these providers has a highly specialised role in patient care. A physiotherapist helps people get back on their feet and shows them how to be safe when walking and exercising. When I injured my back a few years ago, it was my physiotherapist's patient and dedicated input that helped me heal. I remember talking to him about his decision to choose physiotherapy over medicine. He told me that he found elite athletes fascinating and had long harboured a dream to work in their environment. He was training in sports injuries and, after a few years in the profession, had begun to work with swimmers and long-distance runners. He described a sense of achievement from helping elite athletes achieve their goals.

Occupational therapists ensure that people are safe in their homes and can manage their daily activities to keep them functioning. They advise people about home modifications and practical ways of making life more convenient. After an elderly neighbour was hospitalised, she told me that she had seen many professionals but the most helpful person was the one who showed her how to use her arthritic hands to open jars more easily and arranged for home equipment that allowed her to shower and walk more safely. My neighbour said that those were the interventions that allowed her to remain alone at home and be content. What better way could there be to make a difference?

When a child stammers and is embarrassed in front of his friends or a stroke patient has to learn to talk again, it is the speech pathologist to the rescue. Someone I know has a child with developmental delay and speech difficulties. He tells me that he and his wife meet the paediatrician once a year and often come away feeling he doesn't engage with them, but an experienced speech pathologist has been a godsend, helping their child improve with communication and helping them cope with their emotions. They are desperate to change doctors but are willing to travel anywhere to stay with their speech pathologist. I found their account humbling.

I was recently asked by a pharmacist to provide some feedback as part of his performance review. As part of the review, I was asked to answer some simple questions such as what I found useful about his contribution and how he helped me provide patient care. I felt that I could virtually write a book to explain how he had made my life easier and made a difference to patients. For one, he had prevented scores of prescribing errors made collectively by doctors. He was exceptionally knowledgeable about drugs and often worked as a ready reference for me in the midst of a busy clinic. He was an advocate for patients and had frequently helped me figure out the most cost-effective prescriptions for the poorest of my patients who were groaning under medical bills. Pharmacists like him possess broad knowledge about medications, interactions and common health conditions; no one should be surprised that they command the community's trust and respect.

Commonly, when people come in to see a doctor, they want to know what's wrong with them but what everyone needs is someone to talk to and help them cope with the difficulties of life. Many people don't necessarily have a medical illness but they need help. A good psychologist can restore the patient to good form and save the community precious healthcare dollars. Psychologists are skilled listeners and take pride in helping people identify coping skills and build resilience. Through patience, compassion and empathy, they help people find a way through their troubles.

I have come to realise that as the population ages and our hospitals are filled with the elderly and very elderly, nearly every patient needs a social worker. I have used the services of a social worker in aid of my patients increasingly in the past few years and the trend is set to continue. Social workers are equipped with a wealth of knowledge about how to help patients navigate crucial problems like unstable housing, stretched finances and social difficulties. They are adept at identifying vulnerabilities that doctors may not even have considered and are trained to think of practically useful ways of helping patients manage in the community. Many times I think that the professional with the greatest impact on the patient's welfare is the social worker.

Paramedics are widely admired for their quick thinking and acts of courage and professionalism. Patients rely on their counsel and in cases of emergency lives depend on the minute to minute decisions made by paramedics. When one of my children was involved in an accident, I felt as if all my medical skills left me and I put our care in the hands of the paramedics, who brought method and calm to the situation. Other times when I have stopped to assist at roadside emergencies, I have breathed a sigh of relief when the paramedics arrived.

I left nursing till the last, but not for any other reason than the enormous regard I have for nurses. Nurses are worth their weight in gold and I can't say enough about the care, compassion and solace a good nurse can bring to a patient. In fact, no matter how excellent the doctor, it is the day to day care of the nurse that makes a fundamental difference to the patient's overall experience. A dedicated nurse is the best advocate a patient can have. Nurses help frightened and anxious patients raise their concerns with their doctor; they bring attention to critical things like hunger, pain and insomnia; they are more likely than most to sit with a patient, hold a hand and ward off fear and anxiety. Every holiday I am reminded of the power and influence of nurses when the cards and gifts to the nurses outnumber mine by the dozens!

Nurses serve not only hospitalised patients but also those in the community. Maternal and child health nurses make home visits to ensure newborns are thriving. Palliative care nurses, whom I work closely with, visit dying patients in their homes to keep them comfortable. Infection control nurses keep the community safe by ensuring appropriate use of hygiene measures. Psychiatry nurses deliver care to the mentally ill. The list continues. It's no wonder that nurses occupy a very special place in the hearts and minds of the community.

All of these professions and others I may not have touched on in the realm of healthcare are a meaningful way of making a difference to society. The initial qualification is gained in a shorter time with a less intense curriculum, but there is room to grow in each profession and gain higher qualifications. It's important to view these professions not as 'better' or 'worse' than medicine but as worthy occupations in themselves.

Many students want to become a doctor because they say they love science. An enjoyment of science is an important aspect of being a doctor, but the practice of medicine is often equal part art and science. It involves talking to patients, caring for their concerns, being involved in difficult and sensitive negotiations, looking after seriously ill and dying people and having the mental strength to deal with all of this on a recurring basis.

If you are passionate about science above all, you should definitely think about a career as a scientist. I have met a few doctors who realised part-way through their medical course that what they were really, truly interested in was the science of medicine. They liked the idea of working in the lab, designing drugs, discovering molecules, finding new treatments, dreaming up new ideas. They didn't hate the patient contact (or sometimes did and dreaded the patient encounters), but what got their juices flowing was answering a scientific question through research.

My friend Keith was someone like that. Keith was brilliant, funny and warm. He also hated seeing patients. As soon as he got to the clinical years of medicine, the patient contact wore him down. He became disengaged and depressed until one of his professors recognised the change in him and urged him to take time off. Keith was afraid he would never return to medicine if he did that, so he plodded through the clinical years and then into a compulsory year of internship. He was capable, kind and never unsafe, but he received poor references because his lack of interest in clinical medicine was obvious.

Fortunately, he kept in touch with the professor, who convinced him to spend a year in research. This year would become the turning point in his life. Suddenly, in the quiet and studious environment of the lab, Keith blossomed into the scientist he always was. He surprised everyone by making an important discovery early on in his career and publishing his work in one of the world's most prestigious journals. Now his work is globally recognised and his research continues to make a real difference to patients and their doctors worldwide.

After many years, Keith decided to return to a little bit of clinical work to keep his skills alive, and to be inspired by the beneficiaries of his research, but his true love remains the lab. Some medical students and doctors leave clinical medicine altogether to pursue science, while others try to have a foot in each world. Medicine actually needs both kinds of doctors – doctors who are part clinician and part researcher but also those who bring their medical training to a career dedicated to scientific research.

However, it helps to figure out early why you want to study medicine and if your aim is really to be a scientist, whether pursuing a science degree and dedicating yourself to a particular stream of science, for example, biochemistry, pharmacology or physiology, may be your best fit. For this, it pays to talk to pure scientists as well as doctor–scientists, whom you will find at most academic hospitals.

I can't say this enough times but before you set your sights on becoming a doctor, talk to people. Be curious. Even if you are sure you want to study medicine, go out and talk to other health professionals and find out what their work is like. Maybe something you see or they say will trigger your imagination and make you want to learn more about a career you hadn't really considered. Choosing a profession sounds like such serious business that it's quite a revelation how many people end up in careers through serendipity.

Talk to your parents, your school or university counsellor and write down a list of pros and cons. Doing these things will help you define a clear sense of purpose in your own mind, which will in turn make you a more assured candidate when applying to medical school.

3

How smart do I need to be?

'The art of medicine consists of amusing the
patient while nature cures the disease.'
Voltaire

With an acceptance rate of less than 5 per cent, the extremely high grades you need to get into medical school will be familiar to you. This applies whether you study medicine in Australia or almost anywhere in the world. The grades are high, seemingly impossible, yet every year thousands of students make the cut. After all, medical schools wouldn't exist if there weren't students.

Make no mistake, strong academic aptitude is absolutely essential to studying medicine. The bar for entry is extremely high and most medical students are at the very top of their class. School counsellors point out a worrying trend where students and parents are failing to recognise that they fall very short of meeting the entry criteria for medicine. Some parents are convinced that academic achievement depends largely on effort rather than innate ability. They insist that their child will simply work harder to meet the standards, even when this is unrealistic.

One parent commented on her two children's ability to enter medicine with welcome frankness. She said that no matter how hard he worked, her older son simply did not have the ability for superior academic success. He had trouble mastering information, had a short attention span, and had always been an average student. His sister had promise but was unprepared to work hard and did the least possible study to pass. She told them honestly that, on current form, they should not apply for medicine, physiotherapy or other medical sciences-related courses that they sometimes talked about doing. This conversation ended up being a useful way forward for the family. Her son chose a course that favoured his interest in sports management; the daughter took time off to decide.

However, for students with strong academic aptitude and the initiative to work hard, medicine can be a great route. Medical knowledge is so vast that no one can master every corner of it. Therefore, there is endless room for curiosity, discovery and re-discovery, and intellectual stimulation.

It might make me sound like a nerd, but some of my happiest moments are spent reading medical journals and being awed by the offerings. And I am not talking about cutting-edge research conveyed through complex statistics that I struggle to understand. In fact, constantly reading medical journals in print and media is how I am exposed to brilliant articles and expert viewpoints, as well as soaring poetry, inspiring narrative and even striking artwork.

My children often ask why I always have a pile of journals at my bedside. The quick answer is that I need information at my fingertips to treat my patients, but to be honest, I also enjoy reading the journals for the sake of reading them. To treat my patients capably, I spend several hours a week reading and learning. There is no test or exam on the horizon for me, but the idea of lifelong learning really appeals to me. As a doctor who advises medical students puts it plainly, medicine is for people who love to study. I agree and would add that students who find studying a chore and can't wait to be finished with it need to rethink their decision.

Having dealt with the fact that you need to be very high-achieving and possess a fundamental love of learning, let's now spend some time talking not about how smart medical students need to be but what their work ethic is like.

Students who get into medicine and thrive are hard-working. They are not all blessed with natural talent that makes them understand things more easily or remember them without effort – actually, such people are rare. Instead, they have decided that they want to study medicine and have figured out what it will take to get there. They pick their subjects accordingly, are organised and dedicated.

They spend long hours studying, but are strategic, too. They work out what to study and how to study effectively. For example, it doesn't pay to spend six hours at the desk if your attention is drifting and you are not sure what you're even learning. Instead, talking to your teachers and to students who got into medicine might give you a plan. It's better to spend a sustained 45 minutes on a topic, take a short break, and return. The most important attribute in my opinion is perseverance, the ability to apply yourself to a task and stick to it. It trumps being 'smart'.

Alisha, a paediatrician colleague, recently groaned that she hates it when people tell her she must have been smart to get into medicine. What an odd comment, you might think. But I know what she means. I'd feel self-conscious too. I identify with Alisha, who says things never came easily to her. Her natural instinct leaned towards the arts at school and she found science subjects difficult to understand intuitively.

Through various stages of high school, I remember failing a few maths tests, dropping out of advanced chemistry and dreading physics exams although my dad is a physicist. Like Alisha, I was better at biology, although not at the top of my class. But I knew that doing well at those subjects was an essential stepping stone to medicine, so I didn't quit. I started again, in a lower level class where necessary, and worked my way up. I had a few books and guides but no tutors. Mainly I applied myself to my school work. At one point, I was so frustrated by my lack of aptitude for maths that I spent two hours a day after school solving maths problems. I learnt two things from this. One, that what was not instinctive could still be learnt through practice. Two, I would make for an unhappy mathematician.

In medical school, I was surprised (and secretly relieved) to meet other people like me, who said they didn't have a 'scientific brain' but they had worked hard throughout high school, particularly the last two or three years, to allow for this.

Something I wish I had done less of is struggling in private. I had formed views about what I was good and bad at, but I wish I had sometimes asked my teachers their thoughts on how I could improve. I wish I had asked my dad to spend more time with me explaining basic scientific concepts that I didn't grasp. But in my teens, I was more concerned about establishing my independence and was probably too proud to ask for help. What I failed to realise is that identifying the barriers would have made my task easier. If you know you want to study medicine, don't be shy asking for help to do well.

By the way, not seeking help and believing I should be capable of understanding things on my own was a trait I carried into medical school. When I struggled with a subject,

I doubled down and did far more work than anyone else I knew. I assumed that if I didn't understand anatomy, or had trouble with lung physiology, the answer was not to knock on a professor's door, but rather to take twice as much time. I now realise that this was unproductive. However, my hard work did result in improved performance every year and I graduated with honours and a smattering of prizes. The lesson I took away is that there is no substitute for hard work, but having a strategy is smart.

Meanwhile, there was no shortage of genuinely smart people in my medical school, some of whom had been assessed as gifted and talented when young. These students, too, had combined their intelligence with hard work to get in but, once they were in medical school, some of them decided to relax. They began to spend a lot of time exploring campus life, going to newly opened bars, enjoying car-racing, video games and doing the things that they felt they had missed out on while studying for medicine. In one way, this was completely understandable but unfortunately, it came at the cost of their grades.

Some of them went from being at the top of their school to needing supplementary exams. I recall listening to their anxieties on the eve of exams when they would promise not to put themselves through the stress again. Some of us were surprised at the risks these students were willing to take, but what I learnt is that it wasn't their innate 'smartness' that had evaporated, it was their application to work. They had let slide the very things that had got them the grades to get into medicine – regular work; strategic studying; commitment to a goal. I was puzzled by this at the time but now I am older, I recognize that these students were tiring early because they had been in the race for many years, sometimes since middle school.

Many doctors observe that the hardest part of medicine is getting in and I would agree. It takes slightly different skills to get in, make it through the course and be a successful doctor. But if you have the aptitude for it and you are willing to combine it with hard work and sound strategies, you can get there.

4

What's the best type of doctor to be?

'He is the best physician who is the most
ingenious inspirer of hope.'
Samuel Taylor Coleridge

My friend Sabina had always modelled herself after her
grandfather, a prominent surgeon. She had fond memories of
spending her childhood with him and accompanying him on
his rounds; some of her earliest words were the names of the
surgical instruments he showed her. Through medical school,
it was accepted that Sabina would be a surgeon and she took
obvious pride in following in the footsteps of her adored
grandfather. When her family would confidently introduce her
to others as a future surgeon, I would experience a pang of
envy that I had no idea where I would end up.

But Sabina's first job as a surgical trainee dissolved her
dreams. It turned out that while she had always liked the sound
of being a surgeon, she hated the work. The hours were long and
the on-call unpredictable but she could put up with that. What
she really hated was the male-dominated scene of surgery,
where she was exposed to snide comments and sexism. She
told me that not all surgeons were like that and she had a
supportive mentor, but there was a distinct men's-club-like
environment that she hadn't expected. The surgeons she met
were nothing like her gentlemanly grandfather.

Nonetheless, she persevered through one year of training and went on to the second year, where things didn't improve. One of her female colleagues was pregnant and Sabina was astonished to find some surgeons criticising her behind her back for making a foolish decision that would impact her career. Recently married, and pondering the best time to have children, Sabina realised that becoming a surgeon was no longer her dream. The next year, she began training as an intensive care specialist, a career that has served her happily.

We both knew a young doctor, Hari, who had always been interested in obstetrics. He would spend hours poring over obstetrics textbooks and imagined himself happily delivering babies until he grew old. He was very excited to enter a diploma of obstetrics but, as the year went on, he reflected that the year was wearing on him and he didn't enjoy his job as much as he'd thought he would. He became anxious when looking after high-risk pregnancies and spent sleepless nights over mistakes he might have made. Then, an obstetrician at his work was sued for negligence when a child he delivered was born with severe brain injury. This event completely shook Hari as he watched the toll it took on the obstetrician and her whole family. Hari managed to finish his diploma but subsequently entered general practice, where he felt happy co-managing patients with the local obstetrics team.

If you are on the verge of entering medical school, the message is that you just don't have enough information to decide what type of doctor you will be. And frankly, this isn't a question you should worry about even though it might feel like you need to have an answer for yourself or people who want to know. Almost certainly, your goals will change with practical experience.

When I was a first-year medical student, a public health professor asked how many of us saw ourselves as working in the developing world. Three-quarters of people's hands shot up. Years later, you could count on one hand how many people ended up doing so. Why? It's not that all those students were engaging in wishful thinking, but the reality changed. When we became interns, and had the opportunity to work abroad, many people decided that they wanted to pursue specialty training, which required them to stay put in a major hospital. Those attracted to general practice also required another stint of training. Some people fell ill, others became engaged, some needed to pay off a mortgage, others had to look after sick relatives and so on.

I see the same phenomenon in rural students. Many students, especially ones who hail from rural areas, feel a sense of commitment to rural medicine, but the reality proves difficult. Sometimes, they are attracted to a training program that is only offered in large cities. Other times, their partner can't get a job in a rural region; they fear that their children don't have the same educational opportunities; or they are discouraged by the relative lack of healthcare resources in rural regions, which puts an additional burden on rural doctors.

What you should know about every single type of doctor – surgeon, physician, GP, anaesthetist, psychiatrist, paediatrician or anyone else – is that no one has the perfect job. There are downsides to each job, but ultimately people do what they do because, on balance, they find they enjoy the upsides more than they dislike the downsides.

When I started medical school, I had no idea what type of a doctor I wanted to be. Internship is an opportunity for an up-close experience of different rotations. I enjoyed most of my work but didn't look forward to being in the operating theatre. I didn't like the smell or the tension of surgery and I found the doctor–patient interactions too short and abrupt for my liking. This is all it took for me to rule out surgery, because I knew there were other things I enjoyed. Then, I toyed with the idea of doing emergency medicine, psychiatry, and some other things, until I did a rotation in oncology.

As I have mentioned, an oncologist advises people about cancer management and usually accompanies the patient on a journey of many years. Oncologists prescribe chemotherapy, manage pain and other common symptoms and provide advice about difficult subjects, including the end of life. While the cancer sufferer is the patient, a good oncologist recognises that, in fact, cancer is a stressful experience that affects the whole family, which calls for a special mindfulness towards others.

My only experience of cancer was the death of my grand-mother in India. I was just eleven years old at the time and mostly recall the sadness we all felt at her impending death. But I had never even seen her doctors and as a result, was neutral towards the career of an oncologist.

The previous resident enthused that it had been a great job, but not for her, just as I knew I wasn't going to be a surgeon. At the start of my oncology rotation, I never imagined that this would be the career for me either, but the months I spent as an oncology resident were unforgettable and life-changing.

I loved the capacity of oncology to deliver the excitement of science with a human touch. We treated patients with ever-changing drugs and therapies but also practised kindness. I saw that compassion helped patients almost as much as drugs.

I met an inspiring oncologist and I never really looked back. Things came full circle when I finally became an oncologist and came back to work for him.

I still look back and marvel at the serendipity of it all. You might think that one's life as a specialist might be more deliberately mapped than that, but in fact, many of my colleagues ended up in their careers in a similar way. We went into study with an open mind, worked hard, stayed curious, and eventually had a gut instinct that we were suited to a particular kind of medicine. Most people who were convinced they knew exactly what they wanted to do didn't end up doing it.

Sometimes it's a good thing not to know your mind until later. Being decisive very early might sound impressive and even give you a sense of security, but really, there is no need to decide what type of doctor you want to be. What you want to focus on is whether you want to be a doctor at all, and then, how to do it well.

5

How long does it take to become a doctor?

'Art is long, life short, judgement difficult,
opportunity transient.'
Johann Wolfgang von Goethe

Important question. Okay, are you ready?

Of the friends I studied closely with, it took us between ten and twenty years *each* to get to where we are! Let me explain. I will start with Liz, who became a GP. That was six years of medical school followed by four years of additional training. Things have changed somewhat and it's likely to take more time now to become a fully qualified GP. Once Liz entered general practice, she upskilled in additional areas like skin care and women's health through workshops and seminars. Now she stays up to date by attending conferences and reading online journals.

Compared to general practice, most specialty training takes several years longer. Let me begin with my own experience. After finishing high school, I studied undergraduate medicine which lasted six years. Internship and residency were followed by specialist training, adding another six years. While doing a full-time residency, I studied for nearly eighteen months to sit a national exam that allowed me to enter specialty training.

Unlike high school or medical school, studying for this exam was particularly challenging because I was also working full-time. I had to manage work, a new marriage, housework and intensive study. If previous exams had needed organisation and motivation, the specialist exam outdid them all. I used the same skills as previously – I had a clear goal, studied hard, took the advice of those who had gone before me and collaborated with a few friends. I will never forget the day I passed because that same night, I attended the emergency department having developed severe gastritis through the stress of the exam and the associated wait for results!

My specialty training lasted three years, which felt like very little for a job with great responsibilities. Many of my colleagues undertook further training, usually a master's (two years) or a PhD (four or more years), while I decided to do something different and opted for a year-long fellowship in medical ethics at the University of Chicago, where I was a Fulbright Scholar.

At the end of twelve years of schooling followed by twelve uninterrupted years of hard medical education and intensive training, I had the *minimum* level of training required to become a specialist. At this point, my non-medical friends had been earning an income for some years. Flushed with joy and relief at the prospect of joining their ranks, I realised with a thud that I could not find a full-time job because there were too many qualified doctors and too few opportunities. It reminded me of getting into medical school all over again.

I have now been a specialist for nearly fifteen years and I have never stopped studying because of the need to stay up to date in the rapidly changing world of medicine. I attend conferences, follow journals and still devote a significant part of my week to keeping up with the latest medical developments. After all, patients deserve this from their doctor.

For students entering postgraduate medicine, a three- or four-year course is followed by four years of medical school and then further training. Training programs vary in their duration, exams and complexity and you can get a sense of this from looking them up. Minimum training ranges between three to six years, but minimum training these days just isn't enough.

Entry into any training program is competitive, some extremely so. There are a set number of places for trainees each year and, depending on the specialty they wish to pursue and how many places are available, doctors can spend several years simply trying to get in. This obviously prolongs the duration of training, especially when the years spent trying to get in are not accredited (recognized) by the specialty college. In other words, you gain experience but it doesn't count towards the formal requirements. Time thus spent can delay life events such as marriage and starting a family.

Once a doctor is accepted into a training program, the rules tend to be quite rigid. A trainee can't say no to working in a certain hospital, going to a rural area or being sent interstate. Being married, pregnant or having young children are not considered valid reasons for avoiding inconvenient placements. You can be separated from a partner and family members for months or a year at a time. Holidays and on-call commitments are determined according to other people's needs too. Overtime work and undertaking independent study and project work is an expectation.

All specialty programs require assessments. Many have exams mid-way through or before exiting the program and there is no guarantee of passing each exam at the first attempt. Able, articulate and reliable doctors routinely miss out on passing specialty exams – it's the nature of the exam. Studying and resitting exams must be undertaken in one's own time, usually while working long hours. Hospitals are not especially sympathetic to these needs since patient care can't stop. And finally, for the trainee who has cleared all hurdles, jobs don't just lie in wait. Like everywhere else, a job takes merit, connections and luck. It's increasingly difficult for newly minted specialists to find substantial employment, leading many people to undertake further training, not necessarily by choice. The difference between medical school and subsequent training is that doctors earn an income while training. Nonetheless, all of the above things add years to training time that few people initially think of.

If you are considering studying medicine, you should put aside at least a decade for training, and expect there to be more. It's worth emphasising that all these training years involve serious, hard work and setbacks and progress depends on good results, not merely 'time served.' I imagine all this sounds daunting, but it's better to know this up-front and be prepared.

I was lucky to get into the specialty program of my choice and pass my exams at the first attempt. I married at what was an appropriate time for me, and was able to have children despite a few setbacks including the loss of a late-term pregnancy. When I was contemplating medical school, I could hardly see myself into such a distant future but what I can tell you is that the time was largely enjoyable and filled with valuable learning, good friends and meaningful experiences. It reminds me that when you have purpose, hard work doesn't seem so bad.

6

What if I don't get in the first time?

'It's hard to fail, but it is worse never
to have tried to succeed.'
Theodore Roosevelt

A few years ago I met two unhappy students who had both failed to enter the graduate medicine course. They both came to see me to seek career advice. The first student, Mia, was very disappointed. She thought she had studied hard and wondered if the exam wasn't suited to people like her. She was a high achiever who had finished a biomedicine degree with good grades. Her closest cousin was a doctor and, judging by how much he enjoyed his work, she had always wanted to follow in his footsteps. She studied hard for the entrance exams but just couldn't seem to crack them.

When I asked her to reflect on why this might be, she ventured that while she loved the factual and science aspects, she didn't feel so warm towards the people side of things, and perhaps this was showing up in the way she answered her tests. Her first failed attempt had only made her more determined to 'prove them wrong' but the second time had led to more soul-searching and she felt that at the bottom of her heart, she didn't really want to be a doctor who treated patients. The idea of medicine appealed to her, patient care did not.

35

She revealed that she hadn't even bothered looking through her test feedback to see why she had failed. She felt embarrassed on behalf of her family to concede this but gradually, we talked about the wisdom of her realisation that medicine wasn't the right career for her. It's actually not uncommon for someone to fail at something before thinking more deeply about their choices.

The second student, Shahid, demonstrated this ability. He had had a difficult adolescence, with his mother falling seriously ill during the most important years of his high school. Being the eldest, he had to help his father look after his younger siblings and simply couldn't find the time to study. His school-leaving grade was very good for someone in his circumstances, but unfortunately not good enough to get into medical school. He looked into other health-related courses at university, but decided that his heart was in medicine. He enrolled in a health sciences degree and did very well. However, he narrowly missed out on his entrance test, once again because his mother took ill.

He was disappointed, but it was instructive to see how he handled things. Shahid clearly looked upon the result as a setback but not a reflection on his ability. He knew in detail where he'd gone wrong and had a plan to fix the gaps. He explained that through his mother's experience he had developed an intimate understanding of illness and wellbeing, the vulnerability of patients and the important role doctors played in the lives of patients.

'I know I can be a good doctor,' he said earnestly. He didn't have to convince me. Shahid re-dedicated himself to studying and the following year won a place at multiple medical schools.

Once he had the marks to make it to the interview round, I am certain that he would have interviewed strongly.

Each year, medical schools attract thousands more applicants than they can admit. Assuming your grades are in the vicinity of the cut-off, you may still fail in your first attempt. Universities look for a mix of candidates and have complicated rules by which they determine who gets in. For every student that gets in, there are more than a hundred who miss out. Having interviewed many high-achieving students who don't make the cut, I privately rue that they would have made fine doctors, but unfortunately schools have to draw the line somewhere.

As I have told you, I just squeezed into medicine, for which I am very thankful, but really I have no doubt that there were numerous candidates who could have replaced me.

Failing to get into medicine is not just a reflection of your skills, a lot depends on the luck of the draw. If you don't get in once, take the opportunity to reconsider if this is what you really want to do. It's okay, and even wise, to change your mind.

But if you are determined to get in, give yourself credit and spend some time thinking about what went wrong. Were you short on an area of knowledge? Did you over-analyse things and get tied up in knots? Did nerves affect your performance? You may be studying the right stuff but in the wrong way. Ask other people what they think they did right, learn from their experience and tackle the admissions process again with self-confidence. There is a profusion of training courses and coaching workshops to help you get into medicine but in my view, no one should feel pressured to take on this additional expense and it is absolutely possible to get into medicine without them.

I was recently asked to speak to a young man, Justin, who was becoming depressed at his repeated unsuccessful attempts to get into medical school. He had sat the graduate entry exam three times and was chastising himself for being a failure. I told Justin that, at some point, it was legitimate to ask how long he would keep trying and whether further tries would really improve his performance substantially. I was surprised at his response that no one had put it like this to him before.

Some students consider studying medicine in foreign countries that may have a less stringent requirement for grades. Remember that medical qualifications are very difficult, if not impossible, to transfer across countries. Most countries require foreign medical graduates to sit qualifying exams again and these exams can be tedious as well as costly. Moreover, after having been a clinical doctor for a few years, it's hard to go back to relearning the basic material required to pass qualifying exams. I have seen many doctors, for example, who have not been able to re-qualify to Australian standards and have made the decision to stop practicing. This is a very difficult and emotional decision. Therefore, if you want to study in another country but then return home, it is important to do your research and find out if this is practical.

After seeing a psychologist and talking to his parents, Justin decided that he did not have the endurance to sit the entrance test again. He took some time off before being accepted into a pharmacy degree. The last time I spoke with him he was happy, satisfied with the difficulty level of the course, and feeling well-adjusted. He told me he had initially been disheartened but had worked through his disappointment to look forward to a productive career.

My advice to anyone who has tried and failed to get into medicine is to re-evaluate your goals honestly and realistically. It's okay to work differently, persevere and keep your dreams alive but, at some point, it is wise to accept that a different career beckons.

7

What if I made the wrong decision?

'If you do not change direction, you may
end up where you are heading.'

Lao Tzu

This is one of my favorite sayings because the older I grow, the better I understand its truth. Since mistakes and mis-steps are so common in life, it's useful to know how to deal with them.

The first thing to say is that medical school turns out to be a reality check for everyone, and in retrospect it can be amusing.

Here, I am reminded of the first time I 'failed' a test and wondered that maybe I wasn't cut out for medicine. It was the first term of my first year and I had to write an essay in a class that is etched in my memory: Health, Illness and Human Behaviour. I have since forgotten the topic but I remember a few weeks later looking at the posted results and finding out that I had scored a mere 65 per cent, which was just above a pass grade into credit territory. I was flabbergasted, sure that the examiners had made a mistake. At school, I had been used to much better grades.

But the bigger shock arrived as I scanned the rest of the results (posted by student ID, before the time of personalised text messages!). It hadn't been a 'low-scoring' test! In fact, many people scored well and truly above me and I saw marks in the range of distinctions and high distinctions. Yes, there were some just passes and a couple of fails too, but they didn't interest me. I was flabbergasted that so many other students were better than me.

Did you notice that? These students hadn't just *scored* better than me, my mind told me they *were* better than me. There was my inner voice saying I didn't belong. I felt dejected for weeks after this. I was too embarrassed to talk to anyone, but did confide in one friend, who breezily brushed off my concerns. Easy for her, I thought. She had got an 83, seemingly without effort. I talked to my older brother, who had finished university by then and had no doubt experienced his share of disappointments. These things happened, he sympathised, but it didn't mean I couldn't do better next time.

A few months later, I faced my first end-of-term exams. I did well on many subjects, but again I was confronted with a new low mark, this time in Microbiology. I felt thwarted by bad luck. I liked Microbiology and was good at it in class, so what went wrong in the exam? This time, I built up my courage to see the examiner. The examiner was kind and helpful – she showed me how my answers had been lacking in depth. The best-performing students had shown they could entertain other possibilities. I saw immediately what she meant and felt sorry for having wasted her time.

Throughout my first year, it took events like this to show me that I was not the best student in my class, in fact far from it. I didn't find this puzzling or astonishing, but I did worry. I wondered whether this spelled the beginning of future, bigger struggles with coursework and whether I should have considered a less demanding course. When I put all my experiences side by side, however, I realised that if I removed the matter of exams I was enjoying studying medicine. The subjects were varied, my teachers were interesting and my fellow students were nice. Most days I was filled with awe at learning something else remarkable about the human body and I loved the interactions with patients, where I came alive.

This helped me talk myself out of my dejection and focus on learning. The next year, to my surprise, I won a faculty prize for academic achievement. The following year I didn't. Then I made it to a shortlist but got pipped at the post. I had to get used to the topsy-turvy world of nail-biting and breezy experiences set together! Each year, there were high grades mixed with not-so-high grades. In my final year, a paediatrician told me, 'I hope you won't mind me saying this. You are very good but the other student in your group is exceptional. She just gets it.'

Did I mind? How could I not?! But by now I was five years into the course and, while his comment stung a bit, I had learnt that my class, like every other, was filled with excellent and talented students and it was unrealistic to stay on top of all subjects at all times. Medical students were not used to anything other than exemplary marks – making peace with anything less turned out to be as important as it was freeing. Not focusing on scholarly pursuits alone allowed me to make room for understanding the human element of illness and learn the nuances of being a good doctor, which was far more than being a top student. I learned to accept that there was room for more than one good doctor in the world. I wish someone had explicitly taught us this at the outset, as it would have saved me, and presumably many others, a lot of unnecessary stress.

After hearing about my experience, let's talk about the reasons students want to leave medicine.

Some leave in their very first year because the work of getting into medicine has been so arduous and the journey so long that they collapse at the finish line. These are students who have been preparing to get into medicine from the time they were nine or ten years old, largely under the influence of their parents. They entered coaching at an early age, sat countless practice exams before the real one, attended university open days and even before they finished high school asked questions like 'What is the best way to become a neurosurgeon?' These students never stopped to think about the why, just the how.

Other students leave because they have unrealistic expectations (like I once did) but never quite come to recognise it. They are high achievers who suddenly find themselves swimming in a sea of similar people and find it hard to cope with the notion that they are not the absolute best. All through school their worth was measured by their grades and there was a linear path to progress. There was a limited curriculum to master, they knew how to compete and how to get an edge over their classmates.

But medicine is messy and human life is nuanced. There is no one way to study medicine or to excel. There are students who intuitively understand anatomy but struggle to make eye contact with patients and there are those who are the most natural talkers who need a hand at the microscope. Medicine really is both science and art and nobody is similar, let alone perfect at both. The lack of stratospheric grades in medical school isn't a reason to leave, rather an invitation to deal with your unrealistic expectations before they become your undoing, for I can guarantee you they will.

Medical faculty bemoan that many students discover that the hype of a medical course doesn't live up to their expectation. They find that they had been so focused on getting into medicine because of its pride of place amongst university courses that they didn't examine the details. They discover that they like one or two aspects of it but not the rest. They think physiology is cool but psychiatry makes them uncomfortable. Or they like the patient contact but don't enjoy the mountains of learning. Or they can maintain enough interest for half the week but the whole week drains them. Alas, medicine is a complete package and the curriculum is designed with little room for flexibility. Which means you have to get good at tolerating the bad with the good.

Every year there are some students who enter medicine who are far and away brighter than the rest of their cohort. They may have been identified at an early age as exceptional or gifted. They enjoy getting their teeth into a challenge and love nothing more than the novelty of the toughest obstacle they can tackle. Getting into medicine is yet another one of those challenges, but once they are in they realise that the day to day life of a medical student is actually quite mundane. It consists of mastering piles of knowledge that isn't immediately relevant, going by all kinds of established rules and respecting hierarchy. For many years, they aren't in control of solving problems and, when they do encounter challenging situations, they realise that an intellectual solution only gets them partway there, the rest relies on human skills.

Intellectually gifted doctors who lack warmth, empathy and compassion struggle to connect with their colleagues and patients. Whether the humanistic qualities so important to medicine are innate or can be learnt is a question that arouses robust debate. My own observation is that people with insight and interest will seek out tools for self-improvement but those who lack insight are left behind. While everyone accepts the importance of good doctor–patient communication, medical schools and hospitals have found it difficult to devote the subject the attention it deserves because of a very crowded curriculum.

Becoming a doctor is at heart an apprenticeship. The subjects are not impossible but obviously they aren't easy and there are really very many things to learn. Some things can be baffling. For example, I was driven to tears in my human anatomy class because I found it very hard to visualize the relationship of muscles, nerves and blood vessels by looking at bottled specimens. This made me envy my friend who excelled at the basic sciences until I noticed how he struggled to master clinical skills like talking to patients and making them feel comfortable during examination. Some of my colleagues were naturally articulate while others found their heart racing when they had to make presentations on rounds.

To some students, the environment and the style of learning feels stifling. These disappointed students leave because medicine hasn't lived up to their expectations – but if they had taken a closer look, they might have realised this earlier.

Mark was one student who switched to information technology after a few weeks in medicine and it seems that this is where his heart had been all along. He told me that no sooner did a lecturer begin discussing the origins of liver disease than he knew that he was in the wrong place.

Two years into medical school, Rita got married, had children and never came back to her studies. I once ran into her at a playground and she told me about being a mother and working part-time at a call centre. She looked genuinely happy. Ten years later, I saw her again. By then, she was happily working in her sister's business. 'Medicine was just too hard for me, I should never have done it!', she laughed, without a tad of self-consciousness. I admired her honesty.

Nik finished medical school but directed his energies towards building a successful business in architectural design. He was one of the happiest and nicest students I knew – and he would have made a fine doctor – but he found his passion in running a business and makes his clients very happy.

Someone else I knew left just months before getting her medical degree because she could not see herself being a doctor. There was intense pressure on her to at least complete her degree in case she regretted it in the future, but she followed her instincts and never looked back. She had children, devoted herself to the parent-teacher association, and found fulfilment in it. Her husband agreed that leaving medicine was a good decision for her.

Lastly, some of my fellow students fell seriously ill and unfortunately their physical or mental health simply did not allow them to continue intensive medical study. I lost touch with a handful of friends when they never reappeared after a semester break. Some spent time in and out of hospitals and rehabilitation, serving as a reminder to all of us about the vagaries of fate.

Every story is different and layered, but the bottom line is that, if you are genuinely unhappy, it's okay to leave. This can happen anywhere in the long continuum of being a medical student to training and being a practising doctor. Remember that episodes of doubt and disillusion are common and almost expected.

You can work through these episodes with the help of self-reflection, professional counsellors, and your friends and family. Sometimes, taking a break or a gap year can help. But nobody's interests – including the patients' – are served if you are chronically unhappy.

The only reason to study medicine is because you *want* to be a doctor.

8

My parents want me to be a doctor

'Care about what other people think and
you will always be their prisoner.'
Lao Tzu

After wrapping up a speech to a high school convention, I was signing books when out of the corner of my eye I noticed a student standing shyly in the corner. When other students offered her a place in the queue, she declined and kept standing. She waited until everyone had left before approaching me. 'I am sorry to bother you,' she haltingly said until I reassured her that I had time to talk. 'My parents want me to study medicine, but my heart is not in it', she burst out, as if she could no longer contain her thoughts. The expression on her face and this one sentence laid bare the battle she had fought all year long.

Her parents were migrants to Australia. They had left everything behind to flee their homeland and their jobs, though comfortable, lacked their old professional standing. She knew that their chief source of comfort now was the lives they were providing for her and her little brother. They worked multiple jobs to send her to a good school and constantly encouraged her to study hard and get into medicine. They said that medicine was a prestigious and secure career. If she became a doctor, she would never need to depend on others.

The girl's face fell as she continued. 'I mean, what they say makes sense from their point of view and I really feel for my parents, but I just don't think I can commit to studying for another ten or fifteen years.'

I asked if she had tried talking to her parents. She replied that she couldn't bear to dampen their enthusiasm. The fear of disappointing them had kept her from raising the issue but, now that she had to select her subjects, she could no longer stay quiet. She explained that she wanted a career in science, not medicine. She had a good relationship with her parents, but on matters of education they were the boss.

I sympathised with her predicament and told her she wasn't alone; in fact, her story was particularly common from students of migrant background. The good thing was that she had already decided medicine was not right for her and had thought of viable alternatives. I suggested she had to find the courage to talk to her parents and involve her school counsellor, who she mentioned as understanding.

I must say that the student looked so forlorn that it was hard for me to suppress the urge to say, 'Here, I'll talk to your parents.' In the back of my mind, I remembered a cartoon in the bathroom of my medical school that implored students not to study medicine for their parents, its creator perhaps a student like her experiencing enduring regret. We didn't find a solution to her dilemma that night, but I hope that our conversation gave her the strength to pursue the path she wanted.

Modern parents are much more closely involved in the lives of their children than previous generations. Recently, I came across a seven-year-old child explaining to another what a 'helicopter parent' meant. A helicopter parent is one who hovers over every aspect of a child's life in the hope of shaping it just right. With people having fewer children and having them later in life, there is tremendous pressure to ensure that the children turn out well. My friend laughingly relates a quote from another parent to her child, 'You will grow up to be a doctor, a lawyer or a failure.'

Modern parents devote enormous amounts of time to selecting the right school, finding tutors, locating scholarships and fostering useful contacts. The child's exam is their exam and it's quite common for parents to sacrifice enjoyable activities, limit their own social lives, defer family vacations, and take leave from work to support a child through the exam season. This support includes things like waking a child up on time, ensuring nutritious meals and clean clothes are available, driving a child to lessons and making sure there are opportunities for relaxation in the midst of intensive study. As the mother of three children, I am sympathetic to all of this and myself grapple between helping a little and doing too much. But with such overt investment in their future, it's no wonder that many students feel guilty at the thought of letting their parents down by choosing the wrong career.

It's telling how many parents concede their own stress because their child is intent on studying medicine when they have never exerted pressure on the child to do so. 'Just so you know', a parent insisted, 'I really don't mind what she does and have never forced her to study medicine.' These parents feel judged by others and wonder if they have somehow been sending the wrong message to their child about their expectations. What I conclude from these conversations is that settling on a course and future career is stressful for both student and parent.

Loving and respecting your parents does not mean fearing them and being unquestioningly obedient. A feeling of duty towards your parents can co-exist with establishing your independence. You are not letting anybody down by following your heart – chances are higher that you will help people this way. In fact, evidence shows that children do best when their parents mix strictness with support and guidance with generosity. Children who are forced into decisions by their parents have lower levels of satisfaction and a greater sense of alienation from family. The belief that intense academic pressure during childhood and adolescence will lead to greater achievement and hence a happier adulthood is false. If you have decided that you don't want to study medicine, for whatever reason, I recommend making this clear to your parents. Rather than throwing hints, you should tell them. It can be a surprising revelation to parents who had assumed that, given their child's excellent grades, medicine was a certain choice.

All parents want their child to be successful, well established and secure. Parents fear that, in an era of job instability and automation, their child might miss out. Migrant parents who have faced obstacles in their own life are driven by the desire to shield their children from a repeat. Amidst upheavals in other professions and industries, the job of a doctor has always been secure, respected and lucrative. In many cultures, academic achievement is a proxy for good parenting. But it is okay for your parents to hear that medicine is not the right career choice for you and that you will make them proud in other ways.

Most parents, once they see the strength of their child's belief, do understand. They feel responsible for your welfare, but ultimately they want to see you happy. Don't underestimate the value of having as many talks as it takes to help them appreciate your point of view and enlist others, including your teacher, counsellor, siblings or another trusted family member.

Some students deal with parental pressure in another way. They have the high marks but they deliberately sabotage themselves at the interview. I have seen this myself in some of the years that I have interviewed aspirants to medical school. Usually, interview candidates are slightly nervous and stiff, knowing the high stakes of their interview. But when one young man came in, he slouched in his chair, avoided eye contact and answered my questions in a nonchalant and irrelevant way. I knew he could do better, but his whole manner suggested he didn't care, so I decided to pause the interview and ask if he was okay.

'I'm fine. I just don't want to be here.'

'Then why are you here?'

'My dad made me come. My dad is a doctor and he thinks I should be one.'

I was astonished by his frankness.

'And what do you want to do?'

'Accounting. I love accounting, but my dad doesn't understand why.'

'I am sorry.'

'Don't be. I *will* study accounting; it'll just take time.'

The bell rang. The interview was over. He had successfully failed it. I wondered what kind of reception he would get at home once his father discovered that he didn't get into medicine despite the marks. No amount of coaching or coaxing was going to convince him to emulate his dad, but what a waste of time and energy for everyone.

Afterwards, I was so confronted by his situation that I discussed it with a senior faculty adviser. She told me that unfortunately there was no perfect safeguard to protect such students from getting far into the selection stage and that it was up to students and parents to examine their motivation to study medicine before that point.

I have heard of parents who dangle the carrot of financial support if their child studies medicine. Medicine is amongst the most expensive courses to study and medical students and even young doctors need to rely on their parents for longer periods than other graduates. However, mere financial support to study something as taxing as medicine without having an interest is a bad idea.

I have heard some students and parents say that young adults don't have the maturity to make decisions that will impact their future in unforeseen ways. There is probably some truth to this – I thought I knew everything at age 18 and realised every decade thereafter how wrong I was – but the way to gain maturity is through experience and making one's own mistakes. Entering medicine is a significant decision that should be led by you, the person doing the work.

Speaking from a parent's perspective, there is one thing that I have found extremely attractive about medicine that few other careers offer and it isn't something I appreciated until I had my own children – flexibility. Medicine is an exceptionally flexible career where it's possible to work a few days, find job satisfaction, earn well, and balance work and family. The price of this is decades of studying, and even then, depending on what you choose, whom you work with, and where you live, part-time work may not always be possible.

If you are facing parental pressure to study medicine, what I can tell you is that you shouldn't do it if your heart is not in it. Studying medicine and surviving as a doctor is hard enough when you are dedicated, but if you are doing it to make someone else happy, chances are you will end up unhappy (and so will they.) The rates of anxiety, stress, mental illness and self-harm are higher in the medical profession than in the general population; this appears as early as the first year of medical school. You owe yourself self-respect and self-care.

So, although dealing with parental pressure can be awkward, or downright difficult, giving in to the pressure will make things harder in the long run. Be honest with yourself and ask if *you* are prepared to make the kind of commitment that medicine requires.

9

Will I miss out on fun stuff?

'There is no substitute for hard work.'

Thomas Edison

My life between the ages of 15 and 32, the period between high school and completing specialty training, was spent mostly buried in books. Don't get me wrong – I also had fun, made good friends and managed to keep in touch with almost all of my close relatives, who still speak to me! But it would be untrue if I said that becoming a doctor came without significant sacrifices to my social life.

Like many medical students I speak to today, I missed out on many fun things and had to be carefully organised to join in the things that were important. In high school, I took advanced science and maths prerequisites, which as I have said before I wasn't naturally good at, so I had to work doubly hard to get good grades. What fuelled me was the knowledge that if I got into medicine, I wouldn't have to repeat those subjects.

Having narrowly made it into medical school, I felt extra pressure to maintain form. My classes in the first couple of years were staggered, with lots of free time in between. But while the other university students (especially in the first years) sunned themselves in the quadrangle, exchanged stories, and made plans for the weekend, the medical students could be seen to eat quickly and rush to the library. It's not that the other students never worked – of course they did, and the ones that went on to do well were very studious – but it was clear that the demands on a medical student were of a completely different and more absorbing nature. The stress of even a first-year medical student was apparent.

My textbooks were very expensive and I shared a house with friends. To help pay my bills I had a part-time job, like many university students, but my classes didn't allow me to work during the week so I usually worked the weekend shift. One of my more interesting jobs was working as a research assistant in the hospital. I greeted patients when they arrived for their tests and tabulated their health data. I felt that my interactions with accomplished health researchers taught me much. But I still have a warm spot for my long-term job at a bakery, which taught me how to deal with all kinds of people. I also learnt to be patient, punctual, and not judge the type of work people do for a living. This last lesson is critical to my work as a doctor.

After I finished my shift, I would usually get together with friends to study, going through the week's lectures and preparing for the week ahead. The medical course covers an enormous amount of material at a fast pace. There is no defined chapter or book that you can read to say you are done. It was as true for me as it is for today's students, who have more content and more sources to contend with.

There are no regular quizzes, infrequent homework and very few, if any, long assignments, so this means that staying on track is the student's responsibility. For extended periods, no one asks you what you are doing. You can study the bare minimum or learn something properly, knowing that this may be your only chance. Unsurprisingly, the most consistent students were usually less stressed at exam time. But, like everywhere else, there were students who undid the wrapping on their textbooks the night before the exam, stayed up the whole night and prayed that they'd get through!

I have been asked if I resented 'giving up' my life to medical studies. Certainly I was aware that medical students needed to work extra hard, but I liked medicine so much that it was hard to resent it. Being surrounded by similar people who cared about becoming good doctors was enabling. I do think university life has changed since I was there and many more students are working hard to make ends meet and to figure out how best to divide their time.

The best tribute I can pay to my medical school is that when I graduated, I felt prepared to work as a doctor under supervision. I knew it was a long road ahead, but I had the basic skills and confidence I needed to introduce myself to patients and make a start on their care. I never thought I had 'arrived' and to be honest, I still don't, but the criterion by which I judge every leg of training is to ask – do I feel prepared to take the next step?

If there was one notable stress-free period in my life, it would have been my intern year. I loved my work and, best of all, I had money in my pocket! My job was busy and included some overtime, but I loved it. I loved watching my theoretical knowledge come to life, I enjoyed connecting with patients and I thrived on acquiring new knowledge. There wasn't a day when I went to work and didn't come home with a nugget of learning.

The best part about internship was that, on the weekends I was free, I could walk into a bookshop, choose all the books I wanted to read and just buy them! I am an avid reader and it gave me endless satisfaction to be able to buy books without having to wonder if I could afford them. My library grew steadily that year and I am still very fond of those books bought with my new income.

I readily admit that my happy story of internship is not everyone's story. Many young doctors find it a difficult transition from a relatively sheltered university life to demanding real life. Students who have never worked in a job before and have spent all their time studying can find the workplace experience especially challenging. Young doctors have many masters – patients, nurses, and of course, doctors. In order to progress, they must perform well and impress their seniors. In order to find satisfaction and meaning in work, they must do what they think is right. Unsurprisingly, where human beings are concerned, tensions are common in the approach to patient care, division of duties, and personal versus institutional expectations. For example, a common problem for interns (and indeed, all doctors) these days is the pressure to discharge patients when they may not be completely well or to see them in the inadequate allocated time in clinic. Interns and doctors in the more junior phases of training can have a constant feeling of begging for favours and pleasing many parties while combating exhaustion, anxiety, harassment and the fear of doing something wrong that will jeopardise their career. After years of studying, the highly anticipated years of becoming a real doctor can prove hellish. Institutions are doing more than ever to address these problems but no one thinks they are gone.

I recommend doing a small, part-time job during medical school for as long as possible. It teaches you responsibility towards others and introduces you to the array of personalities found in any workplace. It teaches you time management and gives you an insight into your own behaviour, how you manage people and their expectations and how you respond to situations – hopefully, these insights allow you to hone your interpersonal skills while training to become a doctor.

When I finished my year of internship, it was surprising how the pressure came rushing back to decide on a training pathway. I enjoyed internal medicine, the branch of medicine that deals with the prevention, treatment and long-term management of adult diseases, but I was also interested in psychiatry and emergency medicine. Therefore, the year was spent working full-time and trying to figure out where to head next. As I have said elsewhere, the way to find out whether you are a good fit for a job is to get some experience. In the year leading up to my decision, I worked casual and weekend shifts in emergency and other specialties before ruling them out.

Once I had made up my mind to opt for internal medicine there came the applications process. Yes, it was back to competing with very bright young doctors for a limited number of spaces in the training program! At this point, there was no formal exam but references and the interview mattered a great deal. I remember working hard but sweating under the stress of not knowing whether my work would bear reward. I felt under constant scrutiny as I tried to impress those who would decide my fate. At the time, doctors, only a few years older than me, voted to admit their interns into the physician training program. Their say mattered and it was easy to see how a clash of personalities might thwart one's chances. I breathed a sigh of relief when I got in.

Once I was admitted to the physician training program, I started studying again for a comprehensive exam that I think was the hardest of my life. I worked full-time in jobs that demanded increasing responsibility and supervision of interns and medical students, while studying constantly and consistently for nearly eighteen months for two exams, a written and an oral.

While there was camaraderie amongst those of us who were studying, other people including our families could be hard-pressed to understand how any exam could require such intense preparation. But the exam was held once a year and we all knew how important it was to get through at the first attempt, for the sake of our sanity and appearances. There was considerable stigma attached to failing an exam. So we deferred engagements and marriage, slipped out of important social events and spent every weekend studying. I took two weeks off to get married, apologized to my study group for the disruption, and got back to studying as soon as I could. The internal pressure was so intense that even though I knew it was ridiculous, I had a hard time convincing myself that it was okay to take a minor break.

This kind of dedication was not unusual, by the way. It was expected and the only way not just to pass an exam, but actually gain the knowledge that would form the framework of becoming an able physician. We all worked hard; still, some of my colleagues didn't pass and had to endure the stress of another year, or in some cases two. During this time, it was common for them to feel demoralized and anxious about whether they would get into the specialty of their choice.

Having passed the exam, I had to find a place in the oncology training program. Again, I faced the search for strong references and the stress of interviews. I got a job and breathed a sigh of relief for the next three years before the hunt for a job as a specialist would occupy my mind. With consecutive challenges, I really hoped that the last one would prove easier!

With the benefit of experience, I now fully appreciate the additional dilemmas faced by today's students. They have to study hard and compete hard. In an era of postgraduate medicine, when students are older, they also have to think about when to fit in a relationship and marriage, having a family, buying a house, and paying off debt. As it becomes more common – and indeed necessary – for both partners to work, doctors need to think about the impact of their job choices on the other. As society ages, more of us will be called upon to care for our elderly parents. Like other people, doctors need to find a way of reconciling their obligations to their family with the demands of their job.

Students are sometimes amused to hear doctors discuss medicine as a lifelong commitment with implications that may not even be on your radar right now. I had very little idea of what lay ahead when I entered medicine but I'd want you to know that you will sacrifice many things that your friends and family will do. You will miss birthdays, weddings and other important occasions. You won't be able to stay out all night and be safe at work. You can't have a fabulous social life and learn all the skills that are essential to becoming a good doctor. You are likely to work many weekends, public holidays and festivals. There is no such thing as a guaranteed presence at a Christmas lunch, an Eid dinner, or a Bar Mitzvah. And despite your commitment and selfless work, not everyone will praise you or understand you and you will draw criticism for not meeting expectations and for being an entitled member of society.

But if you are willing to join the journey, there are also wonderful rewards – the privilege and the pleasure of impacting lives, a sense of satisfaction, and a genuine purpose to one's days. When I close the door and it is just the patient and I in the room, I still feel inspired and somewhat awed by what unfolds. These are the emotions that are at the core of being a doctor.

10

I am interested in two careers

*'Where your talents and the needs of the
world cross, there lies your vocation.'*
Aristotle

As a high school student, it is not unusual to be attracted to
a few career options. In fact, this is a wonderful freedom of
being young, the capacity to dream. When I was in high school,
I really enjoyed writing. My excellent English teacher soon had
us composing university-level essays and critiquing reputed
works of literature. He was notoriously difficult to please, so a
good grade in his class carried serious merit. But it wasn't the
grade so much as the world of learning that his class opened
me up to that made me long to be a writer. In school, writing
assignments sent a thrill through me and I spent hours crafting
essays in my mind and playing with words.

I toyed with the idea of becoming a journalist but I wasn't
so interested in day-to-day reporting as I was in writing occa-
sional long pieces. Having moved countries frequently with my
parents, I was drawn to world affairs and at one point thought
to explore the career of a diplomat. But that too fell by the
wayside, primarily because I had never met a diplomat and this
was before the day of internet research and global connectivity.

I was not one of those wedded to the idea of medicine
since a young age but in high school I found myself drawn to

the idea of being a doctor. I was once badly burnt as a child and I remembered the kindness with which my doctor had treated me.

At the age of eleven, my grandmother developed cancer and I, with my whole family, watched in awe at the power that her doctors wielded. They knew about drugs, symptoms, bodily functions, and even how close she was to dying. If I had one later regret it was the fact that they didn't communicate all that well with my bewildered family, but thirty years ago times were very different and the idea of speaking frankly with family members was not prevalent. I thought that a knowledge of medicine practised with kindness and empathy could be life-changing. I didn't pay attention to what kind of specialist I would become because I didn't believe it mattered as long as I had a steady purpose, which was improving doctor–patient communication.

I had been writing a diary since the age of 11. I wrote in it throughout my school years and when I entered medicine I decided that, despite the busy schedule, I would continue. In medicine, I stumbled on human stories that were better than anything I could ever have come up with, so I continued to write. I documented my life as a young doctor, the sights and sounds of the hospital, my thoughts on medicine and whatever else came to mind.

I dreamed of writing a book but didn't know how to go about it. With the help of a university professor, I worked on a few narratives and the buzz of publication was enough to renew my enthusiasm for writing. I took some more baby steps towards producing essays about the practice of medicine from the viewpoint of a trainee and then a specialist. Some of my essays took several rewrites but I enjoyed the feedback from seasoned editors and treated their criticism as a unique opportunity to hone my writing skills.

It wasn't until I became a fully qualified specialist that I wrote my first book, which was an oncologist's perspective of treating seriously ill patients. Other books followed and now I write a regular column in *The Guardian* newspaper about medicine and society. My writing has also led me to interesting opportunities on television and radio. My radio programs explain medicine in plain language so that people can feel empowered about their own health. I love the process of interviewing people and learning new skills.

Sometimes people ask if I should have chosen the career of a writer, but I think not. As much as I love to write and communicate with the public, and as nice as it is to chalk up writing books (my favourite part is penning the acknowledgements and the dedication!), I am at my happiest treating patients. I don't see medicine as another job but a vocation. There is great fulfilment in service and service is really its own reward. As someone told me to remember, medicine is my passion and everything else is icing on the cake. He was right.

So how do you decide if you are tossing up between two careers? It's easy to say go in the direction you're passionate about, but sometimes it's hard to know – and being passionate about the idea may not translate into liking the reality. Therefore, I strongly recommend going out and seeing what a career looks like in action. I understand you are busy studying and there may not be much time for work experience – however, before investing your life into a career you should make time to find out more.

Some time ago, I received a work experience student sent to me by his parents, who told me that he was deeply interested in medicine. The student had no sooner sat down than he asked me where the information technology (IT) department of the hospital was located! He offered to fix a fault in my computer, wanted to know how the electronic medical records worked and wondered if doctors could do IT. I asked him what he was really interested in and he replied IT, but he felt that one way of pleasing his parents and doing what he wanted to do was to get the medical course over with first. This is the kind of student who might get into medicine but is more interested in making apps and exploring the technology that drives medicine. If you are like him, my advice would be to enrol in a shorter course that teaches you about healthcare and follow your real passion by doing IT.

A childhood friend of mine works for a children's hospital. Although her father was a reputed surgeon, she had no medical leanings. She works for a large children's hospital and oversees the computer system, which is essential to every step of modern medical care. I am touched that she describes the best part of her work as helping children although she never meets the actual patients. A computer whiz kid I know has built a phone application to help patients keep track of their medical appointments, tests and medications. Applications like this can be life-changing for patients.

Developing technologies that help doctors provide better healthcare or make things easier for patients is a very nice way of making a difference. I ended up talking to that student's parents and to his school counsellor about directing him to interesting IT options rather than forcing him to study medicine. His parents sounded surprised but eventually relented.

A second student who came for work experience was said to have wanted to do medicine ever since she was young. At least, this was what her parents told me. She came and sat with me, observed a range of patients, got taken on a hospital tour by an intern, but after a week still could not articulate a reason for studying medicine beyond the statement that she just did. I was struck by her lack of curiosity and at one point, wondered if her family had made so much of her desire to study medicine that she was afraid to think otherwise. To me, this showed a lack of careful reflection and I worried that without strong purpose she would lose herself in the cut and thrust of medicine.

The third student struck me as different from the outset. She wrote to me (instead of her parents or her school doing so) and explained why she would appreciate an opportunity to sit in my clinic. She mentioned that some of her experiences around doctors had motivated her to study medicine but she wanted to be sure about her choice. When she came to the clinic, she asked thoughtful questions about decision-making, about the emotional impact of medicine and what difficulties to expect. She was realistic because she didn't want to gloss over those difficulties.

Some of the things that medical students are attracted to include building health applications, designing health policy and contributing to health systems research. Other doctors become healthcare administrators, lead think-tanks, or work for pharmaceutical companies. It can be said that all of these professions benefit from someone with a medical background, but that background does not have to be a full medical course, which is really geared towards making a clinician.

While no one can stop you from applying to medical school, it's worth having a close think about why you want to study medicine. Is it to use your medical degree as a bridge to something else? Are you more interested in making a global difference rather than a difference at the bedside? If so, have you thought about that 'something else' as your primary course and looking at other ways to fulfil your interest in healthcare?

People enter medicine with lofty ideals. The majority of students see themselves as rescuing refugees, abolishing disease and changing the face of suffering. But the reality of medicine is that most medical graduates settle down in a familiar pattern of medical practice where they see patients on most days and ask the same questions over and over. How are you today? What can I do for you? Where is the pain? What scripts do you need? As a cancer specialist, I don't cure cancer as often as managing its complications. I treat vomiting and diarrhoea, ease pain and listen to patients who are upset about weight gain or hair loss.

Routine medicine, that is the day to day work of medicine, is not exciting or innovative. It is in fact quite mundane and repetitive (with maybe interesting bursts) but importantly it helps patients. Some patients are the beneficiary of cutting-edge treatments but all patients need kindness, patience and empathy. Dressing an ulcer, stitching a wound, mopping up blood and inspecting a stool sample are not ground-breaking stuff. Sitting with a dying patient, holding the hand of a grieving spouse, helping an elderly lady off the floor, aren't either but these are the hundred small acts that constitute medicine.

I will never forget the time that I saw a ninety-year-old patient, in distress due to severe constipation as a result of chemotherapy and who needed a manual dis-impaction, which is a euphemism for putting your hands in the rectum and removing hard faeces. I saw my intern's face expand with horror at the idea when I told her that's what we were going to do. 'I didn't think doctors had to do this,' she whispered. I felt it was unfair of me to expect her to carry out the procedure, so she ended up holding the patient's hand while I gave him some sedation followed by relief from his constipation. Afterwards, the patient cried tears of joy and within days was back on the golf course.

That day, the intern learnt that good medicine is both saving lives and relieving pain and suffering in whatever form it comes. But these daily acts of care and kindness have been known to stump the unprepared. Medical educators observe that the point at which the dropout rate in medicine is the highest is when students transition to clinical placements. Suddenly they realise that most chronic diseases are just that – chronic. They are not curable, not intriguing, and their implications are, in fact, quite messy. The older the population gets, the more the healthcare system seems like a revolving door of people being patched up, only to return again. There is satisfaction, and I believe gratification, in treating these patients, but it's far from glamorous.

Frustrated parents sometimes tell me that their child is being indecisive about choosing a career. But indecision is a sign of active thinking. I wish more students would be indecisive until they have had a chance to explore their options and talk to people about the lived experience of a career. You should certainly not decide on a career in medicine without taking stock of its downsides.

11

Is being a doctor more stressful than other professions?

'Joy, temperance, and repose slam the
door on the doctor's nose.'
Henry Wadsworth Longfellow

I think about this often, especially when I am feeling over-whelmed and lament that I should know to cope better. After all, it's not easy running a small business, being a policeman, paramedic, teacher or social worker. Parents who stay home to care for young children and sick, disabled adults face constant stress too. It turns out that in modern life stress is everywhere. You are stressed if you are unemployed or inade-quately employed and you are stressed if you have a good job and steady income.

But it is well documented that the rates of stress and the consequences of unmanaged stress, ranging from rates of alcohol and drug misuse to mental illness and self-harm, are higher in medical professionals compared to other profes-sionals. Why is that? Shouldn't a privileged job, respect from society and a good income be protective? Having spoken to many different professionals about this, I can identify one key element. Doctors who carry the weight of human life in their hands day after day shoulder an altogether different responsibility.

A friend of mine is a much-loved GP. He tells me that, while he loves his work, he is always stressed about the lack of time to devote to his patients. He feels bad wrapping up a consultation when there are obvious issues that cannot be dealt with in ten or fifteen minutes. But he is also mindful of the people in the waiting room who have pressing issues. He regularly goes home ruminating over his patients, what he could have done better and whether he missed something. Sometimes he worries about missing a life-threatening diagnosis, which could ruin his practice but mostly he rues, he is troubled by his own conscience.

I identify with this. Every day at work, I meet people who are very sick. They come to me with high expectations and hope that I will treat their illness and make them feel better again. They hang on to my every word, structure their day around our appointment and dissect my words and expressions long after I have left. When people are in hospital, they will skip going to the bathroom or having a shower in case they miss seeing the doctor. Outside of hospital, they plan holidays and reunions around major medical events. Even when there is no good medical treatment, patients cling to the hope that their doctor will come up with something. They are not misguided, rather they are being human.

This is when you realise that there are very few binary choices in medicine, where you can say yes or no. Everything depends on the patient and the context. A treatment that is futile for one person may be life-saving for another. Advice that is shunned by one patient turns out to be another patient's salvation. A procedure that you are new to is the one you need in an emergency; ideally, you would get help, but you are on night duty in a rural hospital – you can't shrug your responsibility.

You learn that, while medicine is a team effort, doctors carry a disproportionate amount of power and hence, responsibility. You run decisions over and over in your head because you want to get them right – there are human lives on the line. And even when you can't save people (as portrayed by television dramas), you know that what you say and how you behave has a lasting impact on the patient and the family.

In that way, a doctor's visit is unlike a visit to the shops or the bank. You know this from your own experience. Think about the last time you or someone you know needed a doctor. How much did bedside manner matter? What lasting impressions did you come away with?

If you are a good doctor, you worry about your patients. This doesn't mean second-guessing every decision but being concerned and being open to the possibility that there are things you have missed and that, despite your best efforts, things will go wrong. I will never forget a hospital lawyer saying to me that you weren't a good doctor if you had never been sued.

A few years ago, a patient of mine stopped taking her prescribed cancer tablets because they made her ache and she needed to be pain-free to work as a massage therapist. Two years later, she returned to me when the cancer had spread to her liver. My heart sank at this. My first thought was that I should have been more forceful in my warnings or managed the side effects better. The other side of me said that, as an adult, she was well informed and had had more than one reminder of the importance of taking her pills. But then I knew many patients who had taken their medication faithfully and still developed cancer, so maybe it was her bad luck.

As this monologue continued in my brain, I had a patient sitting before me feeling frightened, sick and no doubt very regretful. My job required me to put aside my personal frustrations and provide her the reassurance and care that she needed.

Things like this happen every day in medicine. People don't understand instructions; they follow instructions and get unlucky; they develop disease for no rhyme or reason; they don't respond to treatment; they respond but their spouse doesn't. The list is endless.

With an ageing population, I meet scores of elderly and very elderly patients who are not only ill but also lonely. They don't see enough of their children or grandchildren; they are upset at being alone; they fear going into a nursing home; and they feel that life is not worth living. There is no medical prescription for loneliness.

The whole of society needs to respond to these needs, but your patients see you as someone they can share their innermost thoughts with even though they appreciate that you can't fix their problem. Not everyone wants to deal with this, however. While writing this book, I met a very funny vet who regaled me with the story of his mother wanting him to be a doctor. He said that his very first day of work experience made him depressed at the row of sick patients and their worries. Still, he applied to medicine and marked his rejection with a private celebration with his friends! Meanwhile, his mother never lost hope that one day he would tire of animals and gravitate to humans.

As a doctor, you are exposed to many needs of patients, only some of which you can fulfil. But the job of a good doctor is to listen and to advocate. No one is trained to meet all of a patient's needs, but it's still important to remember the person behind the patient and provide holistic care. Many doctors get this instinctively but it's very difficult to practise that kind of slow medicine in the current environment when bureaucrats and administrators control the flow of money and resources.

Medicine is taxing also because the fate of patients seems close to home. You may never need a lawyer or an accountant in your life, but everyone needs a doctor. It can be difficult to separate yourself from patients' situations and think that they will never happen to you and your family. Every patient encounter is a reminder of the fragility of one's own life. Doctors need to be reflective and resilient in order to cope with these daily challenges.

I think this is the blessing and the curse of medicine. If you compartmentalise it and treat only the diseased organ, medicine feels sterile and not the kind of work you set out to do. But if you provide holistic care, you are at constant risk of feeling inadequate, caring too much and living many situations as if they were your own. In my opinion, this is the balance that doctors have to get right and this is what gives rise to the greatest stress in medicine.

So, I do feel that being a doctor is uniquely stressful but I also consider that doctors have better access to knowledge, resources and supports than others. The anticipation of stress is not a reason to rule out a career in medicine but it helps to be aware of what to expect.

12

Does your family benefit if you are a doctor?

'The best way to find yourself is to lose
yourself in the service of others.'
Mahatma Gandhi

Many students have a strong sense of filial duty, that is, a duty to one's parents to support them, care for them and make them proud. In some cultures, there is an expectation that a child, particularly a son, will bestow honour and prestige on the family and deliver practical and financial assistance. As global boundaries become more fluid and people travel to far-flung places in search of opportunity, one of the commonest reasons people migrate is to give their children a better life.

A friend once asked me to speak to two girls she had come to know through the local church. Their mother was the wife of a Korean businessman who had sent the family to Australia so that the girls could get a better education. The children saw their father twice a year. While they thrived in school, their mother had a hard time adjusting. She had left her job back home and spent her day doing chores around the house, keeping the garden tidy, and making trips back and forth from school. She would always wave pleasantly but I wondered what her life was like.

When I met the children, the younger daughter, aged ten, spoke first. She told me she knew I was a doctor and asked how old she had to be to join medical school. Her older sister was fifteen and also wanted to study medicine. They both said that becoming a doctor was the only way to repay their parents' sacrifice.

As I heard them talk, I was moved by their thoughts. They reflected that they had 'split up' their mother and father for the sake of their education; they worried about their father, who couldn't cook and ate junk food if their mother wasn't around; they saw that their mother felt lonely even though she never complained.

The strong emphasis at home was on the girls' education and getting into a good university to study medicine. The girls felt it was only natural for their parents to want the best for them and in fact they felt there was no better way to show their parents how grateful they were. Eventually their parents would get old and they dreamed of having a united family with no pressure on their parents to work. Being a doctor seemed like the ideal way to achieve this.

Of course, these aspirations are not exclusive to migrants, but migrant children are often contending with strong parental expectations when deciding on their future. The next month I met a young man from a small rural town who was visiting universities to decide what to do. His mother and father were farm workers, rural dwellers whose desire for higher education had been supplanted by the need to work on their family-owned, drought-afflicted farm. His parents knew no one who had gone beyond high school and made no work demands of him at home because they wanted him to study hard.

It was his science teacher who had sown the seed of studying medicine in his head and encouraged him to approach the solo

GP in town for advice. The student had been intimidated by the thought, but the more he reflected on it, the more he developed a liking for the idea. Over the course of months, the GP talked to him about the varied experiences of being a rural doctor and in the end the student decided that this was where his career lay. He spoke with knowledge about rural disadvantage and his goal of improving rural health literacy and access to services.

Everything he said was mirrored by his personal experience, which made his stance personal and compelling. The final thing he told me was that he couldn't wait to become a doctor so his parents could put up their feet – filial duty combined with self-reflection.

When I applied to medicine, I had not thought of the benefits that would accrue to my family. We were a family of non-doctors, so some of the benefits of being a doctor have come as a pleasant surprise, but I have to say they are not without complications. One purported benefit of being a doctor is that you can diagnose your loved ones. How convenient to have a doctor in the home who can reassure family members about minor ailments, stem a bleeding wound, tell a simple faint from something more sinister, and know what to report to paramedics.

However, one of the first lessons you will learn is not to treat your friends and never be your own family's regular doctor. At best, it's unwise; at worst, dangerous. No matter how good a doctor you are, your objectivity is muddied when it comes to loved ones as patients. Every doctor has stories about missing a diagnosis, unintentionally misleading a relative, of a reaction being either complacent (and dangerous) or exaggerated (and also dangerous).

When my parents migrated to Australia, one of my first jobs was to ensure they had their own doctor. As they get older, they need more medical help, as do their friends. My friends have young children who seem to go through the compendium of childhood illnesses. When illness strikes close to home, the best thing to do is listen but not to diagnose and never to prescribe.

This is a lesson the community doesn't necessarily understand. People wonder why you would make your relative wait in line to see a stranger when you could do the job better. Sometimes there is pressure from family and friends to renew a simple prescription or check out an odd rash, but to do this is to set yourself up for ethical dilemmas. The law also looks harshly upon doctors who treat their family members.

However, one benefit I have enjoyed in medicine is making many great connections. I deliberately use the word 'making' rather than 'having' connections because building connections is a lifelong exercise. You do it because you are curious about people, not so you can get their help later. Good relationships arise from journeying with other doctors and helping them in their time of need. The help is usually not treating that doctor – it comes in the form of covering a night shift, doing someone's weekend, dropping in to see an ill spouse, staying back to see someone's long-term patient for an opinion – but people have long memories, they remember favours and they respond with goodwill. I am also alive to the privilege of having relationships with doctors older and younger than me. Older and retired doctors have listened to me and guided me to find my own path – for me, their perspective on medicine and life has been particularly valuable as I juggle careers in medicine and writing and feel as if I could be doing a better job of both.

I pay them forward by mentoring doctors younger than me, hearing their particular challenges, and reflecting on how the system can better support them. It's reassuring to know that there are people you can confide in and nice to know that you are a confidant to others. These relationships are a buffer in bad times.

After twenty years in medicine, I am proud to say that I can quickly find all kinds of doctors to get advice and on occasion this has been a tremendous advantage, such as when my daughter met with a serious road accident and needed plastic surgery during the holiday season; when my mother became acutely unwell after an overseas flight; or when a relative needed cancer surgery over Christmas. I do think family members feel reassured that there is a doctor in the family. A doctor understands medical jargon, knows how to navigate the system and can (sometimes!) cut through bureaucracy.

These occasions are fortunately rare. Keep in mind also that not everyone welcomes the responsibility of looking after family members. Some doctors feel it's a millstone around their necks because it's stressful and personal. By far the most important reason I cherish my connections is because it helps my patients. There is nothing like the relief associated with finding help when you need it. While the health system by and large serves most people well, the neediest of all patients can sometimes do with extra advocacy. This is when a quick phone call, a late-night email, or the aptly named 'corridor consult', where you stop someone in the corridor to get advice, can make a difference.

I am always grateful for my connections and use them often, always with consideration and with the knowledge that I am ready to give back too. As an oncologist in a major hospital, I regularly receive calls for help from fellow doctors. On routine review, a cardiologist suspected a patient had cancer. The patient was about to go on a long cruise, so the cardiologist called to see if I could see the patient and confirm the diagnosis. I saw the anxious patient the same evening and I know that the appointment and my explanations calmed him.

Days before Christmas, a GP rang about a newly diagnosed patient with cancer who needed emergency treatment. It didn't take long for me to arrange a hospital admission. The connections that doctors make in medicine we mostly end up using for public good, not private benefit.

An important benefit that had never crossed my mind until I became a mother is the flexibility associated with being a doctor. Apart from the intellectual fulfilment and the joy of making a difference, I consider job flexibility as the single greatest benefit associated with being a doctor. Doctors are well known for working long hours. I know specialists who easily spend 14-hour workdays and then go home to dictate letters and check results. Then there is the regular on-call, which depending on their specialty can mean not sleeping or having interrupted sleep. Trainee doctors also work long hours by necessity, in order to complete their requirements.

In 2015, of the 100,000 registered medical practitioners in Australia, 88,000 were practising clinical medicine. The average doctor worked 42 hours a week. Doctors in training work the highest weekly hours with the least flexibility but as doctors grew older, they had the ability to cut down.

As society confronts the problem of work–life balance and becomes more comfortable with not only the notion but also the practicalities of co-parenting and allowing both partners in a relationship to reap the benefits of employment, I think men and women in medicine will consider their choices more deeply.

A few years ago, one of my residents gave up on the idea of surgery because of the impact his long training would have on his wife's medical training and the upbringing of their infant daughter. This attitude would have been unheard of in the past and his decision may even have been mocked in some circles, but he did what was right for his family.

Many doctors are realising that building in some free time during their week is essential to their wellbeing. They make a deliberate decision not to work every day. For some doctors, full-time work is what they are used to, what they thrive on and what works for their family. Some may have a spouse who is a stay-at-home parent, or for whom the financial gains from work are taken up by childcare costs, and who makes a choice not to work. Doctors who are the sole income earners have a greater pressure to work long hours.

What I have grown to appreciate about medicine is that it accommodates people who work seven days and also those who work two days a week. They obviously make different incomes but both have a choice and both can find intellectually stimulating work.

Once I had children, I decided not to return to full-time work. Oncology is a particularly demanding profession. My patients are very ill, often dying, and emotionally upset. Their care involves looking after the whole family and their needs evolve quickly. Even when I was working long hours, I loved patient care (and to be honest, didn't miss the children!), but at home I was very tired. All my children went to childcare, which was positive and practical, but I longed to have them at home a little more.

Being an oncologist meant that my patients gave me perspective. I learnt over and over that ultimately what gives life meaning is our relationships, and not the degrees or wealth we accumulate. Those things provide temporary satisfaction but I never met a dying patient who regretted an honour he didn't get or a book he didn't write.

I wanted to enjoy my career and I wanted to be present for my children. I also wanted to fulfil the jobs of being a wife and a daughter. Women put a lot of pressure on themselves to 'do it all' and society frequently warns against women 'wanting it all', but in truth I was happy with a bit of everything and grateful that a career in medicine would permit me this. I have never lost sight of the fact that this privilege is not available to many men and women who harbour similar aspirations.

Here are the things that I have gained from my flexibility. In addition to seeing patients, I have attended many school concerts, plays, fairs, athletic carnivals and parent–teacher meetings. I have helped school children with literacy, organised school story-writing competitions and been an aide in the classroom. I have stayed home with my own sick children and sat with my hospitalised parents. I have explored new recipes, enjoyed an afternoon walk, and sat outside on a sunny day to enjoy a book.

In the second decade of my career, I have been able to write and think more. The practice of medicine brings up many thorny dilemmas which are difficult to digest in the moment. Having a day off work helps me understand these things, learn from them and become a better doctor. When I am not seeing patients, I occasionally work on the radio or television, demystifying medicine and making medical matters more accessible to people before they become patients. Along with my regular columns in *The Guardian*, these are opportunities to step beyond the bedside and make a larger difference. All this makes for a very interesting life and I am eternally grateful that the career I chose has allowed me to do this.

Here are the downsides. By working part-time, my career has not advanced as far or as fast as many of my peers. I don't have any additional degrees; my work doesn't attract research grants or feature on the nightly news. I have missed out on promotions and on leading projects that I believed I'd be good at. I am not the first name that comes to people's minds when they think of an accomplished oncologist and I don't have a prestigious private practice with a long waiting list. Between medicine and writing many people can't even figure out what I actually do and I am often asked if I am really interested in practising medicine, as if one can rate this interest on a scale. If there is one thing I have learnt about medicine, it is that there is always someone better, more visible, more distinguished, more driven and more articulate than you. It's a good idea to get used to it!

And I haven't even mentioned pay. Working part-time over the most productive years of one's career has a distinct financial disadvantage. In addition, choosing to work in a public hospital rather than the private setting carries an additional financial penalty, which is why most doctors choose to work in both places. There is other value in private practice, including a closer relationship with one's patients, but this choice comes at the cost of inconvenience and difficult logistics.

There is no ceiling as such for a doctor's income – the more patients you see, the more you earn – and it's easy to wonder if you are not living up to your financial potential after having studied so hard for so many years. But the average earnings of a doctor are high and doctors are always in demand, so working part-time is quite sustainable.

To end – if you think that becoming a doctor is good for your family, it depends, and probably not in the way you think. The greatest benefit of a good doctor is actually to broader society and ironically this might come at the cost to your family. It's good to know this before you decide to study medicine.

13

Is being a doctor sad?

'There are only two sorts of doctors; those who practise with
their brains and those who practise with their tongues.'

William Osler

Medicine raises difficult questions for the former, while doctors
who practise with their tongues might feel less affected by what
they see. One of my enduring memories of internship is the
day I was called to review a surgical patient. It was a weekend
afternoon and I was covering a number of wards, where my
job involved keeping patients stable, ensuring that their drug
chart was up to date, fluid orders were complete, and any
new symptoms were promptly reviewed. Many patients were
immediately post-op, and they might have problems with pain,
nausea or breathing. Unless a patient was very unwell, the first
port of call was the intern.

In the midst of these routine tasks, I received a call from
the charge nurse, who wanted me to review a patient urgently.
I ran over to the surgical ward to find first a nurse in distress,
followed by a patient in distress. The middle-aged patient was
seated uncomfortably in a chair with wet bandages swathing
his abdomen. As I watched, the bandages became soaked with
blood and a nurse, with double-gloved hands, gently removed
the cloth and reached out for a fresh bundle. As she was replac-
ing the bandages, I noticed the man's intestines protruding

from a large abdominal incision. The nurse told me that he had undergone emergency surgery a few days ago but the surgery had been unsuccessful. The wound had been left open to drain, but meanwhile other complications had developed. Now there was a low-level continuous oozing from his intestines, soaking the bandages.

The sight of so much blood scared me and my first instinct was to say this problem was beyond my capacity to solve. Before I opened my mouth, the nurse whispered that she was feeling very helpless because the surgeon had just been by, examined the wound, told the patient there was nothing else he could do and left with instructions 'to keep him comfortable', which meant he was dying.

With growing alarm, I recognised that I had a few problems on my hand. One, the patient needed to know he was dying and that his comfort would be ensured. Two, the nurse needed reassurance and support. As a novice, I had seen some dying patients but usually in a more controlled environment, such as intensive care where senior doctors were around, or in hospice, where the patient was already unconscious and attended by family. I had not seen someone quite like this and I didn't even fully understand the problem, but I knew I would have to deal with it.

I sat down with the patient, introduced myself and asked if he understood what was happening. He mumbled something. He denied pain but looked tired and then I realised that he couldn't really answer my questions because his consciousness was beginning to waver. The notes listed his next of kin as his mother. The nurse called her and I sat with the patient until his mother arrived. His mother was ninety years old. I will never forget telling her that her son was dying and that the best thing she could do was to sit with him. The nurse eased the patient into bed, I prescribed morphine and together we watched from outside as a mother gently patted her son into a final sleep.

I only have to walk past that room to be reminded of that day on which my mind had swirled with emotion. I felt angry with the surgeon who had simply walked away, I felt sorry for the unsupported nurse and I felt powerless at my inability to save a patient who didn't even know what was wrong with him and whose mother loved him dearly. Someone should have told me then that this was just the first taste of a career's worth of such feelings. As a colleague would say later, we all walk with ghosts.

The media portrayal of medicine is very skewed. In dramas, television shows and therefore in popular imagination, doctors are handsome, youthful and usually male. They tackle knotty problems, know what to do, and single-handedly save the day. The patient survives, families express their undying gratitude and the doctor basks in approval before hurrying off to solve the next case. I will never forget the time my university friend watched a medical drama on television and breathlessly asked if I would give her a tour of my hospital. I was an intern at the time.

'Can you show me an operation?' she asked.

'No,' I replied. 'I don't have access.'

'Can we go to the trauma room in Emergency?'

'It's empty, thankfully.'

'Then, what do you do all day?'

Her eyes progressively widened and her face fell as she watched me wade through two hours of writing hospital discharge summaries on my afternoon off. 'I thought you had someone else to do that,' she murmured.

Sometimes my character in medicine feels less like Sherlock Holmes and more Inspector Plod. You will be familiar with Sherlock Holmes, the famous detective who had a keen nose for solving mysteries and did so with the unmistakable arrogance of knowing he was brilliant. Holmes also treated his friend and associate, Watson, incidentally a doctor, with casual contempt. Watson was intelligent, astute, humorous and discreet, but was always subordinate to Holmes.

Inspector Plod was a fictional character from Enid Blyton's *Noddy* series of books, which I loved as a child. Inspector Plod always pretended he knew what the problem was and who the offender was. But despite his confident predictions, he could never quite get to the bottom of things. He had a famous catch-phrase to alert you to his superior ability but the words made you giggle because you knew that poor Inspector Plod was often left red-faced, empty-handed and stumped over what went wrong.

I say this a little tongue-in-cheek but a lot of medicine, if not true plodding, really is routine practice. The routine is different for each practitioner, but it is there nevertheless. So a GP might spend a lot of time examining ears, checking blood pressure or adjusting diabetes medications, while a dermatologist's time is spent on skin. As an oncologist, I can't recall the last time I looked into a patient's ears but I frequently have conversations about chemotherapy toxicity. An obstetrician once chuckled that he began his day reading the birth notices while I started with the obituaries.

Even in the emergency department, portrayed as a hive of activity, the large share of patients don't need heroic life-saving measures as much as they need a wound bandaged, a splinter removed, and pain or infection stabilised. As an emergency department intern, I had spent the whole day doing mundane work like treating heart failure and twisted ankles. Once, I was asked to see an unconscious drug-user who had been left in front of the hospital by a stranger. With adrenaline coursing through my veins, I joined the senior physician in resuscitating the patient, only to have him wake up and spit at me for ruining his high.

With each passing year in medicine, I have realised that the media portrayal of what doctors do isn't merely entertaiment, but potentially harmful. It's how people develop misinformed views about a range of things, from the healing power of miracle herbs to the certainty of successful resuscitation (5 per cent in real life, 95 per cent on television).

Most medical students have had little or no exposure to the actual work of medicine. Students with an illness in the family may spend relatively more time inside the healthcare system but even then their dealings are usually from the sidelines, with an adult taking charge.

So let me say that the daily work of medicine is nothing like what you may have seen on television. It is quite ordinary, sometimes tedious, and frequently perplexing, sad, or outright confronting. Saving lives is difficult, impractical and downright impossible in the vast majority of modern chronic disease conditions. Patients are not always grateful, one's colleagues are not always supportive; and one's best efforts often don't seem enough. But there is still a lot of joy in medicine – and it exists in many small acts of service rather than the 'Eureka!' moments of discovery.

I once looked after a university student who was suddenly diagnosed with terminal cancer. All this poor girl wanted to do was finish her studies and look for a good job. Instead, she was hospitalised feeling very unwell and had to deal with questions like where she wished to die and which of her relatives should fly from overseas to visit her because the visa process was long and flights were expensive. These were overwhelming questions for anybody, let alone a student with the rest of her life ahead of her.

Looking after her was an emotional struggle for everyone. It became clear quite early that there was no cancer treatment she would benefit from, but this was a very difficult thing for her to understand and she kept talking about her plans once her 'current problem' was over. I had to tell her repeatedly and gently that she was facing the end of her life. Many doctors and nurses got to meet her and everyone was left feeling emotionally traumatised. Some days she couldn't breathe well, had a high fever, or felt too weak to get out of bed. She was alone and afraid. Her university and some other community members banded together to provide round-the-clock company in hospital, but nothing felt enough.

Her situation seemed dreadfully unfair and we all felt a kind of guilt. Some people wondered if it would be better if she died and felt horrible for thinking like this. Other people felt desperately sad that, in a world full of modern medical wonders, we could not save a young student's life. This feeling of powerlessness is something doctors rarely talk about, but it's universal. What about surgeons? you might ask. Surely they are heroes who save lives. It's true that surgeons can sometimes perform life-saving operations and surgery is very gratifying for the 'fix' it can provide direly ill patients, even when they cannot be cured. In my job, I work closely with surgeons. Even when a cancer is inoperable, I rely on my surgical colleagues to unblock a bowel obstruction, repair a bulging hernia, clean a festering wound, or excise unsightly skin lesions.

These procedures make a vital difference to quality of life and I can see why so many patients hold their surgeon in awe. I hold myself in this category because, when my child was involved in an accident, the surgeon repaired not only her severe injuries but also her fear of looking different.

But any wise surgeon will tell you that performing surgery is more involved than rushing to the rescue. Just because surgeons can operate doesn't mean that surgery will help. In fact, through a range of expected and some unexpected complications, surgery can hurt, impair and even kill patients. I recently met two patients in intensive care who both died as a result of failure to recover from major surgery. In both cases, the surgeon was left wondering whether he should have operated in the first instance.

Another patient survived an operation but her dementia worsened to the extent that she needed to be shackled to her bed to prevent her from falling out. She spent all day screaming in distress and her family was driven to tears by her outcome. When I spoke to the surgeons about her, they were saddened and perplexed. The young doctors were particularly scarred by their role because they felt that by following directions they had made the patient worse.

Many doctors I spoke to reflected that, with an ageing population, many surgical decisions involve ethical dilemmas. There is no right answer, which means that the surgeon shoulders tremendous responsibility for a decision. A neuro-surgeon reflects on the fact that many of the brain tumours he operates on grow back and the initial excitement and relief of the doctor and patient is replaced by anxiety and regret.

A trauma surgeon reflects on coming face to face with road trauma victims where the offender and victim are lying side by side. The victim is critically ill and doesn't yet know that her husband has died in the accident. The offender has miracu-lously got away with a broken arm and leg and a bleeding face. The surgeon knows he must put aside his anger and sorrow to treat both patients fairly, with concern and empathy, but it can't be easy.

General practitioners take pride in continuity of care. It's wonderful to hear their stories of looking after many genera-tions of one family. But amidst the patients who admire and trust their GP, there are also drug-seeking and abusive patients who have threatened and occasionally harmed the doctor. The bulk of a GP's work is dealing with seasonal illnesses such as colds, chronic disease management such as heart disease and diabetes, and a large amount of mental health issues. The challenge is to know a little bit about everything in order to distinguish the minor from the life-threatening. Hidden amongst many medical presentations these days is the real issue of anxiety, depression and stress. The good doctor must listen first, diagnose later.

Non-clinical doctors such as pathologists and radiologists are spared the direct patient encounter but their jobs have dif-ferent stresses. In an era of every patient undergoing far more tests than ever before, doctors are expected to provide results at fast speed. Not every pathology slide and radiology image is exciting or novel. My radiologist friend is a well-known specialist in MRI (magnetic resonance imaging, a sophisticated test). He tells me that most of his overtime is spent reporting the humble chest X-ray, thousands of which are done each day. An eminent pathologist in a large academic hospital tells me that most of his day is spent examining routine slides, but he recognises that they are anything but routine for the patient concerned. What these doctors are indicating is that the largest part of their work is taking care of the ordinary stuff that keeps healthcare ticking.

I hope to have illustrated that the day to day work of medicine is not glamorous and isn't filled with novelties. It is slow, methodical, bumpy, sad, confronting, frustrating and demanding. A good day at work doesn't involve discovering a cure for cancer or winning a big grant. It usually means overcoming some of the challenges of modern medicine to make a difference to someone's life. Sometimes this is by clinching a difficult diagnosis, trying a new drug, or indeed saving someone critically ill.

In every field of medicine, what makes the greatest difference is listening closely, being empathetic, showing kindness and nurturing hope in situations of fear and vulnerability. In many ways, this is the real problem-solving of medicine and why having strong humanistic skills is so important.

Before you prepare to study medicine, it is very important that you get a real sense of what a doctor does. I can't overemphasise this. Approach your GP or local hospital for a chat, or better, work experience. Don't worry if you hear a no – it's usually because doctors have a busy schedule, but most doctors enjoy giving back to the community and are eager to help. Try again and try someone else. An experienced career counsellor recommends talking to professionals at different stages, because an intern's take on medicine is going to be very different from a mid-career professional, whose thoughts will differ from that of a doctor on the verge of retirement. The benefit to you will be a rounded perspective. A nicely worded, thoughtful request for career advice is very hard to turn down.

Ask your school counsellor, parents, or friends for ideas. If you know someone in healthcare, even if it's not a doctor, don't hesitate to ask for advice. Listen to the positive things they say, but pay special attention to the not so positive bits. In this day, with so many available options, no one should study medicine without having an idea of its ups and downs.

14

Do doctors change the world?

'Though the doctors treated him, let his blood, and gave him
medications to drink, he nevertheless recovered.'

Leo Tolstoy

One of the commonest reasons for wanting to be a doctor is
to change the world. These days we all grow up with images
of poverty, desperation and need beamed from distant places
to our nightly screens. Of course, these conditions have always
existed but in the age of social media, countless magazines and
24-hour news channels, the stories are quick to reach us. It's
natural to feel drawn towards helping people who are suffering
and who are worse off than us.

When I was a first-year medical student, this motivation was
evident amongst my peers. The image of a doctor saving lives
in the hot and dusty lanes of Africa or in the destitute villages
of India is an enduring one. There is glory in it and, for those
who succeed, there is meaning. The problem is that the work
is not glamorous. It is more likely to be dangerous, resource-
strained and burdensome, physically and emotionally.

Here I speak from personal experience. My first foray
into global health was a stint of volunteering in India with
Mother Teresa's Missionaries of Charity. By then, Mother
Teresa had died but her organisation was going strong.
Volunteers flocked to Calcutta to work in a variety of places

run by the Missionaries, including a hospice, a medical clinic, an orphanage, a home for disabled children, and a safe house for adolescent young women and older women who had been abandoned, usually for having a disability that made them a liability to their families. All these places were teeming with need. If ever there was a place for a doctor to make a difference, this was it. I even had a natural advantage of being Indian, speaking the local language and being identifiable. As I would soon discover, the reality was far harder.

A health clinic run by the nuns was the obvious place for me to offer my services. Here, numerous people would line up to seek medical advice. These were people who lived in shanty towns or in the surrounding streets under plastic tents. Most had an obvious problem that had worsened during the time they had waited for things to improve because they had no money to see a doctor. Infections were rife and advanced. Sore-infested feet were common from walking barefoot through monsoon rains and rubbish-strewn paths. Children developed external ear infections which had tracked to involve the face. A man who injured his leg in a vehicle accident received an amputation at the local hospital but no aftercare. As a result, his stump became badly infected.

Every one of these infections needed surgical drainage, weeks of intravenous antibiotics and meticulous wound-dressing. None of this was possible through our clinic. We had access to oral antibiotics and we could dress people's wounds, but when they returned to their cramped tents along the streets it was an impossible request to keep their bandages clean and protected from the elements.

I worked in the clinic with a wonderful nurse who would spend hours replicating her Swiss-learnt skills in Calcutta. Rita became particularly fond of a young man with an amputated forearm. He had a wife and two children and worried incessantly about how he would support them. He feared that they would have to resort to begging for a livelihood. He travelled hours by train to see Rita, who was not only his nurse but also his support worker. She listened to him, showed his wife how to bandage his wound, encouraged him to send his children to the very basic local school, and tried to work with authorities to get him the help he needed. But it was all an uphill task. The patient was warm and grateful – and completely illiterate.

Rita and I came face to face with this disempowerment time and time again. It was never simply fixing the medical problem. We had no answer for poverty, lifelong disadvantage, homelessness or malnutrition. Sometimes, when we were very moved, we would pass on a bit of money to a patient, but we knew that it represented a drop in the ocean. On our walks back from work, we often spoke of our guilt and powerlessness and long after we left India, we continued to wonder about him.

Once, the nuns invited me to a rural medical camp. I was given a desk and a chair and brought my own stethoscope. There was a small quantity of medication, mostly vitamins, antibiotics and basic pain killers. When the gates opened, I gasped at all the people who flooded in. It was as if the whole village needed medical attention. Such was the pressure of the work that I barely spent five minutes with each patient. Even if this was acceptable for a quick diagnosis like asthma or diarrhoea, it was blatantly inadequate for anyone who had a more complicated problem or needed to be heard.

The rural camp filled me with misgivings. So many people had come with so much hope, but the rural camp had done little for them. I realised that the camps that worked better were ones that had a particular focus – like checking everyone's blood pressure, vision or blood sugar. Merely making a diagnosis wasn't enough, one had to have the facilities to treat illness. It made me question why the public hospital system in India didn't work properly. Why did people have no faith in their local hospital? Why did people expect more from a foreign-trained doctor who knew so little? As you can guess, I came up with more questions than answers.

To take a break from the medical work, I would sometimes help at the orphanage, which housed young children some of whom would be adopted by European families. The orphanage had permanent carers and the job of the volunteers was to lend them a hand, especially at meals and playtime. After the needs of the medical clinic, it was quite a relief to be around healthy children. It was of course sad to know that they had been abandoned and it was hard to watch one child favoured over another, but it was a better fate than being on the streets.

Again, the reality of the orphanage proved too much for some volunteers and, on her very first day there, a Frenchwoman erupted in rage at the staff, accusing them of mishandling the children and not feeding them properly. She declared that she couldn't bear to work in a place like this, that she had never seen anything like it back home, and took a flight out the same day.

The other volunteers were appalled, but we were all learning that volunteering in poor countries required resilience and coming to terms with our own attitudes. I remember a medical student who confessed to feeling lost in India. He was used to orderliness in his large American hospital and had never witnessed a shortage of anything, let alone essential medications.

Wherever I went during my stint with the Missionaries, I wrestled with my feelings as a doctor. Finally, I realised that the reason I stayed was not because what I did was life-saving, but because it was life-affirming. The patients I saw, the children I pushed on the swing, and the girls I taught, longed for a human touch. They knew I couldn't change their overall circumstances but, for the time I was there, I was interested in them and cared about their welfare. The teenage girls appreciated that I taught them English. One depressed young woman simply liked the fact that I would be her walking companion. The workers appreciated that I wasn't constantly judging them. The nuns liked that I was curious about their life.

Throughout my medical training, I had opportunities to volunteer elsewhere, including in the Maldives after the 2005 tsunami, and the Asylum Seeker Resource Centre, a service based in Melbourne, Australia. Since then, I have spoken to other doctors who have taken time off to volunteer, including those who have worked with prominent organisations like the World Health Organization and the Red Cross.

There are some vital lessons from these experiences. It is logistically hard to carve out time from a professional career to follow your heart. Your usual hospitals, clinics, and even other doctors, are not automatically supportive. Some won't understand your motivation, while others mind the inconvenience of having to cover for a doctor.

There are many rules and customs that guide career progression in medicine; by not heeding them, you can compromise your career. Some doctors wait till they are older and more established before they venture into volunteering roles. Again, this works for some and doesn't for others. Having a spouse, children or dependent parents might deter you from going into rough and dangerous areas. There are financial considerations like a mortgage, medical practice expenses and school fees. And, of course, many of us simply fall into a comfortable pattern of life and let go of dreams from our younger days.

At the same time, I have heard colleagues say of my present hospital, located in a particularly deprived area, that there is not a day we can't look back on to say that at least one person escaped suffering or death as a result of our actions. In the words of one physician, to be a missionary, you don't have to go to Africa. There is plenty of good work to do wherever you are.

My aim is to give you a realistic view of how difficult it is for a doctor to single-handedly change the world. Most students and young doctors make the mistake of not thinking beyond a vague desire to make a difference to some place that really needs it. They're frequently disappointed when their dreams collide with the reality.

I would urge you to think carefully, talk to or research the doctors who inspire you and reflect on whether you have the attributes to turn you from a comfortable first-world doctor into a resource-strained global health worker.

15

Are doctors rich?

'People pay the doctor for his troubles; for his kindness,
they still remain in his debt.'

Seneca

Money is an awkward subject to discuss but an important motivation for many, indeed most of us. There is nothing inherently wrong with wanting to make money and be comfortable, but it's equally important to have realistic expectations.

I was recently explaining to a journalist friend the various motivations that lead students into a medical career when he interrupted me: 'Obviously, it's the money.' I was slightly put off by his bluntness and told myself that it wasn't so. Later that week, I happened to be talking to a paediatrician who told me that his daughter was studying medicine and had jokingly asked why he chose to become a paediatrician when there were so many more lucrative specialties. He went on to lament that many of her friends, in their first year of medical school, had set their sights on the highest-paying specialties – including plastic surgery, dermatology and orthopaedics – without knowing anything more than they featured in the top-paying medical specialties.

The paediatrician then really dismayed me by saying, 'It's all about the money. Many of them are simply chasing the money. They don't care what they do as long as they get rich.' That day,

I really felt his disappointment, because he was confirming something that I was reluctant to believe.

I probably don't need to tell you that doctors are amongst the highest income earners in society. After all, these figures are well publicised via the media and websites that academic counsellors use to advise students about career prospects – and you can always look them up. But what any reasonable person should also know is how doctors arrive at their financial success.

One of my favourite parts of internship was having the money to buy all the books that I wanted to read. I was an avid reader and I loved the sensation of the crisp new pages in my hands. I also enjoyed the feeling of going shopping and being able to afford things. After a tight final year as a medical student, when I had to give up my part-time job in order to study, a steady income was really welcome. My income grew with seniority and in time I was able to afford a house, a better car and other desirable things. Having grown up in a modest household, I was never a big spender. I sought advice from a financial adviser to help me manage my money.

The income of doctors varies greatly by type of work, with procedural doctors typically earning the most. Procedural doctors perform various kinds of interventions, which can range from removing suspicious skin moles, performing a colonoscopy, giving anaesthetic, repairing a hip fracture, or performing a kidney transplant. The level of training, expertise, demand and location of practice are just some of the factors that determine income.

Procedural work doesn't form the bulk of work for many practitioners – specialist physicians, radiologists, pathologists and paediatricians as well as general practitioners come to mind. Nevertheless, these jobs also attract a steady and very good income. Besides, doctors don't tend to have problems finding employment – even in places where there are few other job opportunities – although, as we have discussed, there may be a queue of contenders for the most attractive positions.

It has been clear to me for many years that the vast majority of doctors do very well financially and are in the top bracket of income-earners. Far more importantly, I have learnt that being financially comfortable does not insulate doctors against other challenges in life. Early in my medical career, I met young doctors who had gone into debt from buying fancy cars and spending on luxuries they couldn't really afford, and this probably happens more nowadays due to societal influence. Doctors are also caught up in illicit drugs and gambling, which leads to an alarming loss of money. Drugs and alcohol misuse turns out to be bigger problem than I had foreseen. Money is not an issue for doctors who become addicted to one or both. Every year, some doctors die of deliberate or accidental overdose, but what's telling is how many more live unhappily. Doctors suffer anxiety, depression, problems with sleep and relationships in higher proportions than others. These things impact their health and employment but ultimately affect patient care.

I have seen any number of unhappy doctors try to buy happiness through spending. I have watched them buy private planes, vintage cars, exorbitantly priced homes and luxury holidays on a whim. They have slowly sunk into debt and been in trouble with banks and the law.

One thing people don't realise about medicine is that the income from being a doctor is finite, in the sense that it relies on a doctor seeing a volume of patients. The more patients one sees, the more lucrative it is, but the payment is within boundaries defined by government policies, professional medical associations and ethical obligations to society. The media makes much of the highest-billing doctors 'rorting' the system and individual patients, but in fact the culprits make a small minority and tend to be repeat offenders. Most of the medical profession makes its high income through decades of hard, consistent work. Unlike the windfall from a business deal, a savvy purchase or an inspired invention, making money through practising medicine is a slow and steady process.

I am not implying at all that other people don't work hard for an income – I have never met a wealthy person who has survived on luck alone. However, I have met those whose income trajectory has been different. For example, highly successful writers have spent years on meagre incomes before writing something that broke the drought. Once, at a literary awards function, I sat next to a famous author who had been nominated for a prize. She told me that this was the first year she had not depended on her husband to pay the household bills. She had been writing for two decades and was in her forties. While the public only saw the plaudits and prizes, she revealed how hard she had worked on dozens of books before writing her bestseller.

I know a creative artist who displays his sculptures and paintings at an exhibition every two years. His work seems exorbitantly priced to me (and some of the modern art pieces leave me scratching my head), but his income has to last for the next two years. Then there is the uncertainty of whether the next exhibition will be successful.

If you speak to the founders of successful businesses, they have often spent years tinkering with ideas and have seen little income and many setbacks during that time. People who work in finance have lean years followed by years with a bumper bonus. A banker once told me about his six-figure bonus on closing a deal. The next year, he was made redundant and was having trouble finding a job.

To the extent that medicine is a business, it helps that there are always customers. But high income in medicine is derived from consistent, hard work rather than spurts of productivity, genius or luck. Given their steady, predictable income, banks are eager to lend to doctors, making it easier to accumulate debt. But banks are equally ruthless about wanting their money back, which has caused needless stress and angst to friends and colleagues I know.

Perhaps one of the worst consequences of pursuing money is the breakdown of close personal relationships. When work is rich in financial reward, it's very tempting to pile it on and justify the time spent away from one's spouse, partner, children and extended family as worth it. In truth, beyond a certain level of income, more money does not buy more happiness but does seem to attract more complications.

I know many doctors who regret not having spent enough time with their children or their spouse. One doctor told me that he was on to his third marriage because no one could stand his constant absence from home. Some women lament that they are professionally established and financially independent, but they have achieved this at the cost of a loving relationship or having children.

Financial security in medicine comes after great sacrifice over many more years than other professions. Medicine is not a get-rich-quick scheme. It may not even be a long-term get-rich scheme, if you get side-tracked. It's very hard to practise satisfying medicine if your main goal is money. In fact, a pure focus on money is incompatible with good medicine. If you enter medicine like this you will be frustrated by the realisation that patients with their very human issues take more time than you are paid for. Your patients will be dissatisfied and you will know it from their faces. Importantly, it's a hollow job for a doctor who works only for money. A patient's gratitude, a dying man's blessing, or a family's relief will never seem enough, but this is the real compensation of medicine.

As I mentioned before, there is nothing inherently wrong with wanting to make money, but there are other professions that might allow you to reap greater rewards. Everyone is entitled to a personal philosophy about the importance of money, but my advice is that if you want to be very wealthy look for other ways to achieve this than by becoming a doctor.

16

Will I impress others by being a doctor?

'The fool shouts loudly, thinking to impress the world.'
Marie de France

In a society that judges itself by brand names, titles and possessions, the quick answer is yes, people are impressed by doctors. Saying you are a doctor is really saying a few things in shorthand – that you are well-educated, smart, and hold a position of influence and respect in society. In fact, I would say that this impression goes back to when you tell people you are studying medicine – people already consider you to be a doctor although you are far from it. When I was a brand new medical student, as shaky as they come, I can remember my employer at the bakery approvingly slipping an extra bread roll in my bag and the grocer bragging loudly to his customers that he was serving a doctor! At social gatherings, parents would approvingly recommend me to their children, as if this would suddenly fire their desire to become a doctor.

I remember the warm feeling that I got when I told my friends and family that I had got into medicine. 'Wow, you must be smart!' said everyone, even the auntie who was hardest to impress. It was like an instant badge of approval although I hadn't achieved anything yet and it would be years before I would have any credibility as a doctor. I was simply so grateful for having got in and was surrounded by so much talent that I never thought much of myself. However, I couldn't help but notice that whenever I was amongst my friends or family of non-doctors, I was considered exceptional. At these gatherings, people would single me out. It struck me as odd that they rarely asked about my experience. Everyone assumed it was such a hallowed profession that I must love it; pretty soon, I became wary of even mentioning that there were parts that I simply didn't understand and really wasn't very good at.

At university, too, the medical students were held in awe by others because everyone knew the kind of grades it took to get into medicine. We had all made it to university, but sorting students by course was the simplest way of still judging them.

The most surprising thing I found was that all this adulation, actually led some students to believe they were special. They were not considerate of fellow students or teachers and acted with an air of entitlement. They often had wealthy parents, who indulged them by buying them expensive cars, expensive textbooks (that the rest of us photocopied from the library), and the best of every kind of equipment that medical training required. I remember the parent of one student buying her a costly purebred puppy to keep her company during studying. Another student would be sent on regular overseas holidays to offset the stress of exams.

These students never held a part-time job during high school or medical school because their parents wanted to protect them from stress. Despite their advantages, some of these students failed repeatedly and blamed their tutors. It was a little puzzling to the rest of us that seemingly nothing could take the shine off their self-importance.

Needless to say, the end of medical school and entering into the workforce proved to be a great leveller. Suddenly, we were all at the bottom rung as interns in the hospital. People groaned at the thought of new interns whose knowledge was mostly bookish. The senior doctors had to literally hold our hand. The nurses provided practical tips that would guard us from unintentionally harming patients. The social workers and chaplains, with years of professional and lived experience, smiled tolerantly at our tentative steps. The patients were mostly nice, accepting that we were the most junior of doctors and made mistakes. Astonishingly, they permitted us to practise on their bodies and put up with our fumbled approaches.

Day after day there were many challenges to being an intern, most of them to do with learning the ropes. How to deal with twenty sick patients with as many different conditions; when to persevere and when to call for help; how to deal with grieving families; when to start resuscitating a patient; when to stop resuscitating that patient; when to suspect another intern was in distress, and so on. Every day brought new insights.

One day, as I worked alongside a fantastic intern who had been an average medical student, it suddenly dawned on me that in all my interactions no one asked and indeed no one even cared about the grades I had got in high school or even my rank in medical school. The things that had meant so much to so many people (including me) for so long had suddenly evaporated. Or maybe, I realised, my grades and my university ranking had been something I had been clinging to because it's all I knew. It's what I had absorbed through my school years – good grades meant you were a success.

The truth is you couldn't take one hundred interns and line them up by high school grade or university ranking and predict who was going to make a good doctor. A good doctor combines knowledge with skills like empathy, compassion and genuine interest in the human condition. Top-ranked students struggled to meet internal expectations. Mid-level students suddenly found their footing. Struggling students were not all struggling interns.

The most important lesson I have learnt is that, while credentials are definitely important and tell one part of a story, what really matters is how you treat others. A man in pain will be forever grateful to the person who relieves his suffering, regardless of whether it is a nurse or a doctor. The family of a dying patient doesn't count the doctor's accomplishments, rather the humanity shown to them at a fraught time. Medicine is full of impressive people but time and again patients remember doctors who are, above all, kind. This much about human nature should not be surprising.

Don't study medicine (or for that matter anything) to impress others. The feeling of achievement is hollow, short-lived and ultimately unimportant. What is far more important is a quiet self-belief that you have the right motivation to study medicine. This is the attribute that will carry you the farthest.

17

Should I be concerned about doctor welfare?

'Wherever there is a human being, there is
an opportunity for a kindness.'
Seneca

Having only studied one course, medicine, and worked only
in one career, as a doctor, I have become so steeped in the
culture of medicine that many things seem normal, or at least
like they always were since the time I first entered the hospital
as a medical student. I noticed the problems with the hours,
culture, gender bias, and the misuse of power but I always
told myself that they must happen in every high-performing
workplace.

It wasn't until I interviewed a senior non-medical academic
who raised candid objections that I saw things through different eyes. This researcher had spent many years studying
various work environments, including at top legal firms,
prestigious consulting firms and other successful companies.
She now consulted for a prominent hospital overseeing the
welfare of doctors.

When I first met her, she told me that it had taken her
years to understand the culture of medicine and she was still
coming to terms with the most objectionable things she saw.
She became emotional describing the gruelling shift work and

the unpaid overtime that young doctors regularly performed. But it wasn't the working hours alone, she reflected, rather the conditions of work that broke the back of many doctors.

She would arrive at work early to see doctors sprawled on the floor to catch a nap because there was no dedicated space, let alone a bed. Doctors regularly skipped meals and drinks and there was poor or no supply of food, clean plates, mugs and cutlery in the residents' quarters. Too exhausted to drive after a shift, they had no choice but to return home to sleep before the next shift. No one seemed to care if the doctor was a new parent, had a sick spouse, or wasn't feeling the best – the roster took precedence.

Most of all, she objected, the habit of employing doctors on one-year contracts left no room for mentoring. Doctors moved from one rotation to another, without meeting a stable, supportive figure to help them navigate the difficult journey. She described their loneliness and despair that was sometimes only relieved when they moved jobs. This researcher claimed that in her experience, amongst the top professions, medicine had the worst record of treating its staff.

I protested that this might be an exaggeration, even though I have heard enough stories to suspect she might be right. I asked her what was different about other places. She provided an example of a bank where a late-working staff member would be given a taxi voucher to take her home. Or a consulting firm where you were expected to put in a lot of hours but food, drink and personal safety at night were not a concern. She gave several examples of new employees being assigned a mentor who was actually expected to provide support and feedback. She also talked about regular debriefings to nurture employees and help them find an area of interest. I confess that the more she spoke, the more the realisation hit me that she was right and that I had simply buried my observations by normalising my experience.

Looking back, during my many years of night duty in different hospitals, there was never any room to sit and rest, even if the wards were quiet. The sofas were lumpy and threadbare. By night-time, the residents' area would range from barely tolerable to disgusting, with used coffee mugs, plates, old food and scraps of paper. You might ask why people didn't clean up after themselves – it's because mostly we were run off our feet and would often have to leave a half-eaten sandwich and run to a sick patient. There was rarely any food or drink in the fridge, so a hungry doctor could either buy junk from a vending machine or raid the dry sandwiches saved for emergency patients, which inevitably made you feel guilty.

There was no privacy. If some of your co-residents were loud, watched late night television, or listened to loud music to stay awake, you had to put up with it. Patient care was tiring, but it was the lack of decent respite that made things worse. Some days I felt I would have been a much better person had I been able to put my feet up for just an hour when it was quiet.

It wouldn't have cost a fortune to ensure basic comforts – a clean and organized place, stocked with basic food, fruit, tea and coffee, but it was simply not a hospital priority. Hospitals, public and private, are always complaining of a financial crunch – and the first things to go in these times are small comforts that, once taken away, seldom return. It was assumed

113

that doctors could and would work in any conditions – and so we did, without complaining. On many nights, I got by because a dear friend's mother would pack two meals, one for her and one for me.

It's a common refrain nowadays that working for hospitals feels soulless. Although I hasten to add here that what I am describing is commonplace all across the developing world, where doctors can't even dream of such luxuries when their patients lack basic care.

The work roster was punishing in unusual ways. The people who designed the roster felt it was a doctor's responsibility to switch shifts or exchange rotations but due to the competition for jobs, no one wanted to do this. At one stage, I barely saw my husband for three months and not one doctor would exchange some shifts. It was a bitter consolation that scheduling conflicts also resulted in someone not getting married and another colleague breaking up with her partner. I look back and how realise how twisted that reality was.

I recently met a mature-age medical student who had been in the military and served in recent wars. He told me that one of the things that had surprised him about medicine is how hierarchical it was, even compared to the military. I don't have personal experience of the military but I can confirm that medicine remains a hierarchical profession, which means that it is led from the top. Typically, in a hospital setting, the senior specialist sets the tone, with doctors of varying seniority expected to follow suit.

Medicine is also a wonderful apprenticeship, so it makes sense that someone with experience and knowledge should lead the way; it's when people with power and influence get away with mistakes, unprofessional behaviour, or abuse of privilege that problems occur.

With quickly changing rotations, there isn't the time to get to know senior medical staff closely or figure out their idiosyncrasies. This is a particularly difficult task for young doctors who are learning to be independent but still need strong guidance and backing. They should be allowed to fail and learn from their mistakes, but there must also be adequate safeguards in place to protect against serious harm to patients.

Patient care is fluid, which means that there is often no single answer to a problem. Medicine is a balance of art and science and it can be difficult to get the balance right. Sometimes, on a ward round I am puzzled by why a trainee doctor came to a conclusion that obviously failed to take into account the whole picture. At these points, especially if a patient had been put at risk, it is easy to become frustrated, but I must remind myself to understand another point of view, educate the trainee and try to come up with a plan to prevent a repeat occurrence.

According to widespread reports, a simple error can be the undoing of many doctors, who are subsequently humiliated and persecuted. Bullying and harassment happen because of the power imbalance between senior and junior medical staff, the mismatch of expectations, the pressures of patient care and lack of shared goals. For all the talk about medicine being a team endeavour, the actual players can be highly competitive and driven by personal ambition, which is not surprising if you look at who gets into medicine.

While I have talked mainly about the working environment of hospitals where doctors will spend a significant part of their life, community practice isn't immune to problems. The organisation may be smaller, but the problems are similar, and it can be harder to remove yourself.

This doesn't mean team work is a myth – and in fact, patient care thrives when there is a genuine team approach.

I was recently at a breakfast where someone mentioned that he held one particular meeting of physicians and surgeons in the highest regard because of the doctors' ability to disagree without discord, which led to more considered outcomes for patients. As an attendee at this meeting, I was heartened to hear this.

The public (and the medical profession itself) has never heard more about the corrosive effect of bullying and harassment than in recent times. Whereas doctors were previously expected to put up with things, there is now more serious tackling of the issue, but unfortunately the evidence tells us that bullying, discrimination and gender bias in medicine remain a live issue.

For the past two decades, there has been gender parity at the medical school level, and in fields like general practice, women outnumber men. But in spite of efforts at diversity and inclusiveness, up to a third of women in academic medicine have experienced sexual harassment and these problems have been noted in the earliest years of education and training. Even after accounting for differences, women doctors earn less than men, are much less likely to be promoted, and much less likely to win grants and awards.

I have seen how implicit bias, regarding gender and race, subconsciously drives the behaviour of the community and patients, who might consider themselves well-meaning and respectful of doctors.

Women doctors are less likely to be addressed as 'doctor' and more likely to experience disrespect. As a woman of colour, many patients assume that I am a nurse, attendant, or a therapist until I correct them. When I was a fellow, an elderly woman recalled my male intern and asked what he thought about my advice.

'I don't know that much,' my intern confessed. 'She is my boss.'

'I thought you'd be the head doctor,' she said. 'You're taller.'

Ridiculous as it sounds, this kind of exchange still occurs. My friend is a surgeon of Indian background. When she arrived on the ward to consent a patient before surgery, a clerk mistook her for a cleaner and berated her for disturbing the patient. After a similar experience an African doctor wears a jacket and displays his badge prominently even on the weekend when other doctors are in jeans and casual clothes.

Discrimination and harassment of course have real consequences for the whole of society. They affect medical progress and career opportunities and lead to poorer patient outcomes and patient experience.

It's important to be aware of these things when you are entering medicine. Some people think that you can avoid these experiences if you are smart, poised and confident, but remember that medicine is full of such people and yet they endure difficulties. It's notable and unfortunate that most doctors stay quiet about these issues because they fear speaking up will harm their career. There is truth to this, and these cases are well documented in the media. Workplace discord harms personal health and relationships, and has a deep impact on the ability to provide good patient care. It's hard to be a good doctor if you are an unhappy and stressed person.

During a long education and career spent across several workplaces, nearly everyone encounters some difficult personalities, discourteous behaviour and questionable conduct. Many people will also experience bullying or harassment. The most positive development I can report is that instead of telling complainants to get a thicker skin, there is a strong push and real initiative to tackle offenders, who are warned, educated, placed on probation, and even dismissed. Everyone is taking the issue seriously, which will hopefully lead to a grassroots change.

It is not only abuse from fellow professionals but hectoring from patients that modern doctors have to worry about. Racism and physical and verbal violence against doctors are real. Hospitals, which have many pressing priorities, have traditionally not provided doctors with strong protections against abusive patients, but the rising incidence of drug-fuelled and revenge attacks on doctors that have sadly led to serious injury and even loss of life, has focused attention on the issue.

Some time ago, a drug user slipped into my office while I was on a round, stole my personal belongings and walked off the grounds. I was lucky that I was not in his way at the time. It took time for the law to catch up to him but not before I was a victim of identity theft and spent a year dealing with the consequences. The incident left me reflecting that there was no 'safe place' to even be a doctor, but I am glad to say that the number of positive experiences in medicine have far outweighed the negative and I still feel attached to my work.

I hope you can see that a career in medicine doesn't shield you from the ills and vagaries of society and, perhaps because medicine is known for closing ranks on itself, it can feel like problems are following you. There are system-level challenges and individual offenders. It is important to be wise to these challenges but you should also feel optimistic that there are more avenues than ever before to get help.

However, what I'd like you to take away is the reassurance that much of medicine is filled with good, kind-hearted people of principle and integrity who are a joy to work with and who make the burdens of medicine easier to bear.

18

I am the parent of a student – what do I need to know?

'What you help a child to love can be more important
than what you help him to learn.'
African proverb

The education counsellor was telling me about the pressures that students feel to study medicine. No stranger to these stories, I nonetheless listened with interest and sympathy to the accounts of students fretting over every test and exam, compromising their friendships, and losing all perspective in the race to the finish line, the end of the year exam, not realising that the finish line of getting into medicine, was only the very, very beginning.

The more I heard the more I felt quietly thankful that either my time had been different or that I had been curiously oblivious to such pressures. I don't recall ever thinking that, if I helped a friend, he might take my spot in medicine. And it would never have crossed my mind that, when I asked someone for help in turn, such a calculation would be at play. Even when I look back, although I recognise one or two students who kept their study secrets to themselves, I think the rest of us were very open. We cared about doing well, but didn't think of getting into medicine as a game of one-upmanship.

'What do the parents say?' I asked, somewhat perplexed by the counsellors' descriptions of what her charges were enduring, often over two or three years of high school.

It was the only time her face fell. 'The parents are the problem,' she gloomily declared.

Then the stories came tumbling out. The mother who made her child wake up very early every morning to study for two hours before school started and who had a study plan laid out the minute he came home. The father who had himself failed to get into medicine who wouldn't hear of his son doing anything else. The parent who gave up her job to coach her daughter full-time until the daughter had a nervous breakdown.

The hardest thing, the counsellor reflected, was when a parent had a completely unrealistic expectation of the child's aptitude to study medicine. 'The child is barely passing and the parents say he should study medicine. With the help of predictive charts, I show the parents his expected exam score and how far away it is from the prerequisite for medicine.'

'And does that introduce some reality?'

'No, the parents turn around and say, "Well, he will just have to work harder."'

'And could that be reasonable?' I asked. 'I mean, there are students who don't put in their maximal effort in high school or in a pre-med course. Maybe they need a bit of pushing.'

'Yes, but simply doing more work or putting in more hours is not the answer for every student. Based on their performance, some kids are simply not going to get into medicine and the parents just don't seem to get that.'

I came away with a great appreciation of how hard school counsellors have to work not only to advise students but also to deal with parents.

An educational psychologist I know shared more examples of parents who hurt their children in the quest to make them a doctor.

I was particularly affected by the story of a pre-med student whose desire to study medicine cooled after two years and gravitated towards psychology. Her father, a surgeon, wouldn't hear of it. He reminded his daughter of the work she had already put in and to forget her doubts. He introduced her to various doctors, hoping that someone would renew her inspiration, but never gave her space to discuss her thoughts. Her mother was easier to talk to but had always deferred to her father for important decisions.

The student's choice was painted as a matter of family honour and, in the end, she couldn't bring herself to leave pre-med. She saw a psychologist while preparing to get into medicine and ended up becoming a successful doctor who enjoyed her career. But she had trouble reconciling with her parents' behaviour and felt bitter about their approval based on her achievements. This led to her distancing herself from her parents.

I found this upsetting as a parent and found myself exploring other instances where a child had studied medicine but at the cost of the parent–child relationship. A faculty adviser added his reflections by saying that some of the most challenging cases he had dealt with were those where the medical student wanted to drop out but the parent insisted otherwise. For some students, taking a gap year helped and they came back feeling renewed and committed, but for others taking leave only prolonged their suffering when they were clearly not suited to medicine.

If you are the parent of a student who wants to study medicine, congratulations for having raised an ambitious child. As a parent, I appreciate the hard and often unacknowledged work that goes into raising children. From the moment our children are born, we are driven instinctively to protect them, nurture them and want for them the things that we did not ourselves have. I see this as particularly true of an education.

My own mother was a rare female university graduate in her time, but one who never had the opportunity to work because custom demanded that she look after her family and jobs for women were rare. When I expressed a desire to study medicine, she let me go abroad all on my own at the age of seventeen because she wanted my life to be different. For the next decade, we saw each other once a year during my holidays, which became shorter with time, until my parents finally migrated to Australia when I had my own children.

It wasn't until I became a parent that I appreciated the enormity of my parents' sacrifice and, in particular, my mother's heartache. I hope to be half as wise and strong when it comes to the upbringing of her beloved grandchildren.

Regardless of what really goes on underneath, society doesn't miss a beat when it comes to judging parents whose child gets into trouble or those whose child excels. If your child wants to study medicine, it's natural to feel proud and happy that the decision is a reflection of your parenting. Knowing that you have your child's best interests at heart, here are some things you should be aware of.

There is a difference between supporting your child's decision by engaging in expansive and frequent conversations about why she wants to study medicine and simply pushing your child to become a doctor. Students, whether in high school or in a pre-med course, are young and their maturity has not peaked. If they are doing well, they might feel internal pressure to 'use' their grades to study medicine. You, as the mature adult, should discuss with them the pitfalls of following a career for status or prestige alone and provide them a safe space to discuss their ideas and doubts, what their friends say and what is influencing them.

It's important not to take stray comments as a declaration of intent and hem your child in to a decision. Be open to conversations about wildly different careers. Show curiosity and interest rather than judgement. I recently met a man who could have studied medicine but whose heart lay in hospitality. His parents baulked at the idea of opening a restaurant in an era of ruthless competition, when medicine promised job and pay security. But they couldn't go past his passion and gave him their blessing as well as a small loan. Today, the man runs a bustling restaurant that's the talk of the town and his parents couldn't be prouder. He tells me that the most important thing his parents did was not to lend him money, but to tell him that they loved him no matter what career he chose. This allowed him the emotional security to expand his vision.

In high school, it's a good idea to talk to the teacher and counsellor about your child's ambition and find out what they think. As we have said before, high grades are a critical first step, so it's important to know if your child can realistically expect a shot at medical school or whether you should explore other health-related careers with easier requirements. Also, apart from grades, does your child have the interest in and temperament for medicine?

You may be surprised to find out that the school's perception doesn't match yours, setting up an opportunity to explore why. I remember a high-school counsellor telling me that many tears and battles at home could be avoided if parent, child and school spoke more often and more openly. My children's teacher once told me that parent–teacher meetings should never come as a surprise to parents if they keep talking to the teacher through the year. While teachers are very busy, and parents are no less frantic, if you want to play a role in deciding your child's career, it pays to sit down with the teacher.

Students undertaking a pre-med or biomedicine course at university are slightly older and more independent, but their study is primed with the stress that they have one last chance to get into medicine. Biomedicine students and their counsellors that I have spoken to describe tremendous pressure and competition within the class, leading to fraught relationships and reduced mental wellbeing. Some of these courses are meant to introduce students to other health-related career options, but in actuality the years feel like a rat race to get into medicine. Before encouraging your child to study such a course, have a conversation about this.

If your child is studying medicine, it is important to communicate regularly and know that your child's commitment to medicine remains strong. If you detect wavering interest, it's important not to overreact but to take time to find out why.

Some time ago, I spoke to a third-year medical student who struck me as fine example of a budding young doctor. She was obviously bright, but also articulate and deeply thoughtful. She told me how much she enjoyed medicine and how appreciative she was to have got in. I thought to myself what a pleasure it would be to work with the young woman in a few years when she became an intern. Just weeks later, I was astonished to learn that she was taking a year off.

I wondered how I could have been so deceived by her sunny outlook and if she had been silently suffering. As it turned out, she hadn't been suffering so much as she realised that in all her life she had never had another goal than to study medicine. She had never taken a break at school, had always studied the hardest subjects, and undertaken the least extra-curricular activity possible to focus on her studies. Her parents had always discouraged her from having a part-time job so she could save her energies and they had generously paid for all her needs. Her medical friends seemed all like her.

A year of being on the hospital wards had caused her to think about her life and, at age twenty, she felt acutely one-dimensional. She had trouble relating to patients and talking to them about their interests. She was astute enough to do something – to acknowledge the deficit and do something to address it. In her year off, she took a job at a supermarket checkout and another one at a café. I can imagine the anxiety her parents must have felt but, to their credit, they gave her the latitude to make her own decision and supported her initiative. She had a great year learning life skills and happily returned to medicine.

If you are a parent of a child who is studying medicine, stay open to the possibility of dissatisfaction and burnout starting in the earliest years. A small but still significant proportion of medical students are unhappy, anxious or depressed and it isn't always easy to predict who they are.

As a parent, you can help by being open to all kinds of conversations about what life in medical school is like and by getting to know your child's friends.

It's uncommon for parents to become involved beyond this once a student is in medical school, but if you are concerned about your child's welfare and don't know what to do, never hesitate to call the medical school for advice. These days, medical schools take student welfare very seriously and have dedicated resources for it. Reaching out to the medical school for help might be the best thing you did for your child.

When your child is studying medicine, here are some other issues that can cause stress. Medical students need to study long hours and can seem detached from family members and household responsibilities. Preparing for major exams or interviews might make them seem uninterested in important social events. This can be hurtful to parents and extended family, so make sure you talk about your expectations and review progress.

Due to prolonged studies, medical students may require financial support for longer than others and they often rely on parents for food, transport and other needs. The more advanced years of medical school make it more difficult, though not impossible, to take on part-time employment. I don't think significant employment is compatible with medical school. Despite being studious and organised, I reluctantly gave up my job in final year as it became too much to do. Again, setting expectations and discussing what you are capable of contributing as a parent is important. Not all families can afford to support a university student and you should encourage your child to seek financial advice from the medical school. Some parents help by being a guarantor for a bank loan or making a formal loan to their child. Be open about what you can or can't do and look for solutions together.

Accompanying your child through medical school is not all work and stress! It can be a great insight into an intriguing world of discoveries, breakthroughs and day to day patient care. You will find yourself pulled along into a very interesting world and you will have a front seat position in the journey of young adults as they become full-fledged doctors. Whenever I attend medical graduations, I feel misty-eyed just being an outsider, so I can only imagine the pride and joy a parent might feel on the day. I know that the day I graduated from medical school was an intensely proud one for my family. Sometimes I am embarrassed that my parents still bask in the joy of that moment but I know how much it means to them when I can help someone.

Let me close by wishing you the best of luck wherever you find yourself in the journey. Remember that most of it will be novel and interesting. For your child, a career in medicine has the capacity to be thrilling and inspiring and humbling. Every day will be meaningful in some way. Yes, there will be drudgery and bureaucracy and heartache, but somehow being intertwined with the lives of others will smoothe out the bumps on the long road.

Epilogue

'The two most important days in your life are the
day you are born and the day you find out why.'

Mark Twain

So here we are, nearly at the end. I hope that you have discovered some new insights about being a doctor and you might now be wondering what to do next. Reading this book is likely to have raised thoughts and questions in your mind. Maybe it has confirmed your view that medicine is the right course for you and you feel keen to forge ahead. In that case, good luck and may fortune favour you.

It's also possible that reading this book has raised issues you hadn't even considered and as a result you are no longer sure of yourself. You might feel upset or conflicted or in need of more time to digest your thoughts. It's easy to ignore these feelings and hope they will go away, but I urge you to try and sort through them. You could make a list of questions and share them with people you trust. You could also ask your parents to read this book and talk things over afterwards. If you have been feeling parental pressure to study medicine, sharing an insider's perspective might help your parents realise the truth about medicine.

Of course, reading this book may be the beginning of your exploration, in which case you could make note of things that you would like to discuss further with other people. For example, you could ask your family doctor or other doctors about whether their experiences match the descriptions you have read about here. You might also feel more prepared to explore other areas of healthcare such as pharmacy, social work, physiotherapy, or nursing. Writing some notes to share with your school counsellor might open up a valuable line of conversation.

Now that you have a sense of what a life in medicine is like, you have a framework to ask questions of other healthcare professionals. What is your day like? What is the most satisfying part about your work? What are the challenges? Can I make a steady income? How does career advancement work in your profession? Are there opportunities to volunteer locally or internationally? What are some ways in which your field has changed the world? Would you choose this career all over again? Why or why not?

Reading this book has also hopefully given you an idea of the importance of looking deeply into the career you want to pursue. This means seeking meaningful work experience, being curious, and being thirsty for answers. I can assure you that most professionals are happy to help young people. Some of my most enjoyable days are when students sit in to watch medicine in action. (I am amused at their surprise when a week has passed and nothing remotely like TV drama has occurred on my rounds!)

I often think that I'd like everyone to experience the joy and fulfilment that a career as a doctor has brought me, but the truth is that most applicants to medicine will not gain entry due to the sheer number of competitors. It's important to believe that this is not a sign of failure, because luck plays a part. On the other hand, you may have the grades and not be remotely interested in becoming a doctor – this is a good thing too! Never compete on other people's terms.

The prestige and glamour of medicine are short-lived if you aren't comfortable in your own skin. It's important to know that medicine cannot compensate for other deficiencies. Being a doctor doesn't make your friends or family love you more. Instead, think carefully through your motivation, consider a gap year, and discuss your ideas honestly and fearlessly with people you trust. These steps are more likely to result in a fulfilling career.

Remember that an education is never wasted. If you are unsure about studying medicine, pick another course that you are interested in and reassess things. One of the delights of medicine for me lies in meeting people who have arrived there through diverse paths – from fine art, music and literature to law, pharmacy and nursing. These doctors were first drawn to something else and gave themselves a chance at following their interest and I think they often make for more interesting and rounded individuals.

Finally, you have heard it before but it's worth repeating that your grades don't determine your worth. Neither do the course you enrol in or the career you end up in. What determines your worth is the kind of person you are. Kindness, humanity and compassion towards others are not the sole domain of doctors. Some of the nicest people I know and trust are strangers to medicine. Some of the most helpful people I know have never dreamt of being a doctor. Some of the most impactful and respectable people I have met didn't get to study medicine.

There are many, many ways of making a difference. Take plenty of time to find your way, ask for lots of directions, and don't be afraid of following the path your heart tells you is right.

Here's to your future.

Acknowledgements

While all books feel special, I have particularly enjoyed writing this one because it is my way of repaying the debt I owe to society for supporting me in my work as a doctor in the Australian public healthcare system.

Notwithstanding the challenges, I derive enormous fulfilment and joy from my work, but I have long thought that anyone who enters medicine deserves a balanced appraisal of the life of a doctor while still on the outside. A career in medicine occupies the minds of many but isn't right for everyone. Helping individuals navigate important questions to make an informed choice about studying medicine is an idea that innately appeals to me. Therefore, I have been simultaneously delighted and relieved to find out just how many of my colleagues and friends as well as students, parents and educators, share my vision and have willingly contributed their time and effort towards the making of this book. It is they whom I wish to acknowledge.

Michelle Leech, without whose bold encouragement I may have procrastinated putting pen to paper. From my medical school tutor to a friend and colleague, it is my privilege to know you.

Chris Lemoh, Helen Green, Anu Vats, Julia Harrison, Bernadette Doufalidis, Elizabeth Gordon, Margaret Simmons, Sunil Pandya, Upreet Dhaliwal, Swati Jha, Sophie Van Doorn and Prudence Scott, for combing through initial drafts and suggesting changes both large and small that show how much you cared to get this right. Thank you for being in this together.

One of the nicest things about medicine is the interesting people I have met. Time spent with Gerard Schiller, Wen Shen Lee, Honor Magon, Margaret Hay, Amy Bohren, Yvonne Hodgson, Jon Faine, Mark Siegler, Taru Sinha, Kwai Lee, Warren Hastings and Debbie Nathan have helped me reflect deeply on what it means to be a doctor. Geoffrey and Rosemary Green have poured their wholehearted love and support into all aspects of my work.

This book is enriched by the astute observations of the school students, graduates, professionals, parents, and my own patients who have provided me an understanding of how the medical profession is perceived and what the duty of a doctor ought to be.

I am lucky that Andrea McNamara has remained a steadfast influence on my writing. For good ideas to be transformed into worthwhile books, every writer needs an able publisher. I am genuinely proud to work with Dan Ruffino and Roberta Ivers from Simon & Schuster Australia whose respect for my work and ideals fires my imagination and makes me want to keep writing. Thanks also to cover designer Jacalin King, and to the wonderful S&S Sales team.

To Declan, my most important silent warrior and Anjali, Sachin and Rohan, for your effusive love and generosity, the joy of being a doctor is outdone only by being amongst you. Thank you for illuminating my life.

No book would be complete without acknowledging my parents, Kaushal and Urmila, and my brother, Rajesh, without whose personal sacrifice, deep commitment, and unconditional love, there would be no career and no book.

About the author

Dr Ranjana Srivastava is a medical oncologist, Fulbright Scholar in ethics and an award-winning writer. She is the recipient of the Distinguished Alumni Award from Monash University, from where she graduated with first class honours.

She works in the Australian public healthcare system, where in addition to patient care, she is closely involved in the education, training and mentoring of medical students and trainees. She is passionate about communication, ethics and humanity in medicine, issues about which she writes in her books and regular columns for *The Guardian* newspaper. She is also the recipient of the Medal of the Order of Australia for her contribution to medicine in the field of doctor-patient communication.

Also by Ranjana Srivastava

*Tell Me the Truth: Conversations with my
Patients about Life and Death*

*Dying for a Chat: The Communication Breakdown between
Doctors and Patients*

*So It's Cancer, Now What? The Expert's Guide to What You
Need to Know*

After Cancer: A Guide to Living Well